DEVELOPING
THE LIBRARY COLLECTION
IN POLITICAL SCIENCE

by

Robert B. Harmon

The Scarecrow Press, Inc.

Metuchen, N.J.   1976

Library of Congress Cataloging in Publication Data

Harmon, Robert Bartlett, 1932–
    Developing the library collection in political
science.

    Includes index.
    1. Political science--Bibliography. 2. Reference
books--Political science--Bibliography. 3. Book
selection. I. Title.
Z7161.H268   016.32   75-44396
ISBN 0-8108-0898-6

dedicated to

Ivan and Kathryn Lambert

"And behold, I tell you these things that ye may learn wisdom; that ye may learn that when ye are in the service of your fellow beings ye are only in the service of your God."

King Benjamin
Mosiah 2:17--Book of Mormon

CONTENTS

SUMMARY LIST OF
CHAPTER 3 SUBJECT HEADINGS

PREFACE

Most librarians are aware that book selection is not an easy task. The tools one must use are highly diversified and at times not adequate. Perhaps the foremost problems are recency and authoritativeness. The major concern of the librarian in the selection process is the development of the library's collection to meet the needs of various patrons. It is the selection process that this work addresses itself to in the field of political science. The study of politics is an important one because of its ubiquitous nature and the effect it has upon the life of every individual in society. Within this context libraries play a vital role in the political education of citizens.

The primary purpose of this work is to provide librarians with a selection device for most types of materials in political science. With regard to this purpose it is aimed more specifically at small to medium-sized public libraries, as well as those in junior colleges, and some high school and junior high school libraries. As an auxiliary purpose students and laymen might find this work useful in selecting informational materials although it is not designed to be a guide to the literature.

Selection of works for the core collection was based on reviews and their extensive use in the literature. Others were selected because of the recognized authority of their authors. Each work cited is accompanied by a brief descriptive annotation. No attempt has been made to make these annotations critical or evaluative because all of the materials cited are considered good in their respective areas. It should quickly be pointed out, however, that this work is not intended as a listing of best books.

Thanks are due Professor Irene Norrell of the Graduate School of Librarianship at San Jose State University for early encouragement and suggestions. Special acknowledgment is due my colleagues and friends for their comments and suggestions concerning many of the materials contained herein.

Finally, a special thanks to my wife Merlynn for her invaluable editorial assistance, encouragement, and patience which saw me through.

San Jose, California Robert B. Harmon
May 1975

I. STRUCTURE AND SOURCES

General Note

The subject of politics and government is one eminent-
ly deserving the attention of people at every stage of life.
For example, students need to be exposed to political materials as part of their preparation for the assumption of the re-
sponsibilities of democratic citizenship. Both students and
persons not in school need to keep up with the developments
in politics and government to the end that their participation
will be based on facts and knowledge of current developments.
Moreover, government occupies an increasingly important
part of the spectrum of modern life. Government acts on
and conditions much else around it. Thus to be uninformed
in that area is to neglect one of the keys to understand what
is happening around us. Finally, democracy is based on the
concept of an alert and intelligent citizenry. Although reading is only one way in the present age of mass media to ac-
quire knowledge, it is the easiest for the largest number of
people and so plays an especially large role in the development of an active citizen body.

Chapter One of this section outlines the development
and structure of political science as an intellectual discipline
within the social sciences. It further provides a structure to
the literature of the discipline. Chapter Two describes the
general selection tools for books, periodicals and non-book
materials for the field.

Chapter One

AN INTRODUCTION
TO THE LITERATURE OF POLITICAL SCIENCE

The Development and Structure of Political Science

A serious concern with the problems of politics and government hardly needs elaborate justification today. Political activity is all around us. Politics influences the lives of all of us, regardless of whether or not we participate in the political process.

Politics, Albert Einstein once observed, is more difficult to comprehend than physics. The number of factors directly or indirectly relevant to politics is enormous, and these factors are related to each other in many ways. Political science is both organized and unorganized complexity, a web of myriad relationships among individuals, groups, organizations, institutions and nations. But even webs have patterns, and the search for these patterns is one of the central tasks of political science [The Behavioral and Social Sciences Survey. Political Science Panel. Political Science, ed. Heinz Eulau & James G. March (Englewood Cliffs, N.J.: Prentice-Hall, 1969), p. 11; Chapter One is an excellent discussion of patterns in politics].

Reflections on political things go back to antiquity, possibly to the time an individual was first threatened by a ruler. In Biblical times among the Hebrews the prophet Samuel, about the eleventh century B.C., warned against a centralized monarchical form of government [1 Samuel 8].

12

The results of enthroning a king, he said, would mean war and excessive taxation. Against his urging, the people insisted on a king and received the ill-starred Saul. Politics in ancient Greece, especially as taught by Plato (The Republic) and Aristotle (Politics), was founded on the doctrine that a government was good insofar as it had ethical bases. Politics in ancient Rome emphasized the concept that a government was good if it was founded on legal bases. Political thinkers of the Middle Ages, almost all of them clerical, deviated little from the pre-Christian doctrine of law; however, they claimed that leaders of the Christian church alone were competent to collate man-made law with natural law. Theorists in the area of political science during early modern times eventually withdrew political science and political values from the realm of theology [Thomas H. Stevenson, Politics and Government (Totowa, N. J.: Littlefield, Adams, 1973), pp. 1-4].

Generally by the beginning of the eighteenth century political thinkers judged whether or not a government was good according to some secular base. The question of the individual's relationship to the state is still much with us, and to many writers the wisdom of the ancients still has relevance: "Wherever I go, I meet Plato coming back."

As an instructional field, the study of political science in America can be traced back to Harvard University in the 1640s. Something over two centuries later (1858) a chair in the discipline was established at Columbia, with Francis Lieber as the first incumbent, and by 1900 courses in politics were common. Up to the Second World War, political science was secondary to history in departments of "history and political science." In the meantime, the founding of the American Political Science Association in 1903, and its journal, The American Political Science Review, three years later, were expanding the discipline.

During the 1950s and 1960s a sharp methodological controversy divided most of the field. On the one hand were traditionalists, favoring a theoretical and historical approach. On the other was an approach known as behavioralism. It stressed the politically significant behavior of individuals and groups more than formal structures, abstract theory, and legal authorization. Behavioralism was characterized by (1) a reliance on ideas and empirical findings derived from such other social sciences as psychology, anthropology and sociology; (2) the statistical measurement of the frequency of political actions; (3) an emphasis on the root causes and conditioning factors which may explain political phenomena; and (4) an attempt to develop a "value-free," objective, morally neutral method of political analysis [an in-depth discussion of the development of political science as a discipline is contained in Albert Somit & Joseph Tanenhaus, American Political Science: A Profile of a Discipline (New York: Atherton Press, 1964), and Albert Somit & Joseph Tanenhaus, The Development of American Political Science: From Burgess to Behavioralism (Boston: Allyn and Bacon, 1967)].

The current trend seems away from behavioralism too, toward a sort of eclecticism combining both old and new approaches. Most particularly, there is an insistence that research be relevant to current issues and that it be related to values, to ethical standards of right and wrong. In other words, a systematic description of what is (empirical theory) should be associated with a conception of what ought to be (normative theory) [William A. Welsh, Studying Politics (New York: Praeger, 1973); Chapter One outlines in detail current trends in the field].

As a separate and distinct discipline within the spectrum of knowledge, political science possesses the following characteristics:

(1)   a disciplinary self-consciousness which is reflected in the emphasis placed on critical analysis of the growth and development of the field;

(2)   a body of classic works which stand as milestones in the evolution of the discipline;

(3)   a fostering of specialization within the field in terms of commonly accepted subfields.   Specialists and their subfields may, in some cases, focus on multidisciplinary concerns, as in the case of political sociology and political psychology;

(4)   an easily differentiated subject matter which can be clearly distinguished from that of other allied or related disciplines;

(5)   a body of generalizations or abstractions, parts of which are added, deleted, or modified over time as deemed necessary and appropriate.   These generalizations include the several different types of abstractions appropriate for the development of sound, supportable ideas in the discipline.   They include the following types: laws, theories, principles, hypotheses, facts, values and taxonomy;

(6)   concepts which are peculiar to the field;

(7)   generally accepted and relatively standardized methods of analysis by means of which to confirm or invalidate theories.   This standardization of methods permits all students of the discipline to retest, or replicate the original analysis by retracing the steps taken [Cyril Roseman, Charles G. Mayo, F. B. Collinge, eds., Dimensions of Political Analysis (Englewood Cliffs, N. J.: Prentice-Hall, 1966), p. 4].

Contemporary political science is beset with an increasing number of sub-specialties.   To illustrate the extent of the shifts in interest and emphasis, one need only to look back to World War I to discover that political science then comprised only four recognized subdivisions: American government, comparative government, political theory, and elements of law.   During World War II, the American Political Science

Association listed eight subdivisions: political theory, political processes, public law, public administration, international relations, comparative government, legislatures and legislation, and government and business. In 1963 at the annual
American Political Science Association Convention, the program was organized to reflect the prevailing fields of instruction in the larger American universities. The program
reflected six singular subspecialties in addition to a triple
division of comparative government, thus indicating nine
areas. The areas were: (1) American national government
and politics, (2) American State and local government and
politics, (3) political theory, (4) public administration,
(5) public law, and (6) international relations, foreign policy,
and comparative government which included Western nations,
developing nations, and Communist nations. Since the early
1950s and the trend toward studying the relationship of political science to allied disciplines, there has been an extension
of these areas into further subdivisions such as: political
anthropology, political geography, political psychology, and
political sociology. Thus the focus on the interdisciplinary
nature of contemporary political science.

The Organization and Structure of Political Science Literature

Generally speaking the basic function of literature is
the recording and organization of information. Specifically
the literature of political science is vast both in terms of
its broad subject scope and the sheer volume of current research and publishing. Politics is also a subject which en-
joys a great deal of public interest. Consequently political
science is represented in a large number of libraries of
many kinds, differing greatly in size and depth of collections
and in their availability to potential users.

The study of political science depends on the transfer of relevant information of massive proportions. The information and retrieval devices of the field exhibit a great deal of complexity when compared to those of other disciplines. At the same time significant segments of political information are not transferable because of non-existent or inadequate retrieval devices. Below, in outline form, is a description of the different types of information sources one will encounter in political science. Where appropriate one or more examples of particular works are provided [Robert B. Harmon, Selected Guide to Annotated Sources of Information in Political Science (Morristown, N.J. : General Learning Press, 1975), p. 22].

A.   Documented Sources:

    1.   Books in the Field: Works of this type serve to expound or to systemize or to discuss or to reveal their subject. The forms they take most often are the treatise, the monograph, and the textbook:

        a.   Treatises: A treatise attempts to cover the whole of its subject field. In effect it sets out to be exhaustive, aiming for a complete presentation of the subject with full documentation. There is no current work of this nature for the field of political science generally. However, there are some treatises on specific topics such as History of U.S. Political Parties (New York: Chelsea House Publishers, 1973), 4 volumes, edited by Arthur Meier Schlesinger.

        b.   Monographs: The monograph resembles the treatise in many ways. Traditionally the main difference between the treatise and the monograph is that in contrast to the broad subject scope of the treatise the scope of the monograph (as its Greek etymological origins indicate) is a narrowly-defined single topic. Within its limited subject field, however, the mono-

graph strives to be comprehensive and systematic.   Two examples of monographs in political science are: A. H. Burch, Representation
(New York: Praeger, 1971) and Heinz Eulau,
ed. , Behavioralism in Political Science (Chicago: Aldine-Atherton, 1969).

c.   Textbooks: A textbook is a teaching device.
Its primary purpose is not merely to impart
information about its subject but also to develop understanding of it.   If the role of the
monograph is systematization, the role of the
textbook is simplification.   It concentrates on
demonstrating principles rather than recounting
details.   In political science there are numerous examples of textbooks.   Modern Government, 3d ed. (New York: Dodd, Mead, 1972),
by Dell G. Hitchner and William H. Harbold,
and Fundamentals of Government, 2d ed. (Milwaukee: Bruce, 1963), by Henry J. Schmandt
and Paul T. Steinbicker, are two of these.

d.   Introductions and Outlines: An introduction is
clearly a first book in a subject, designed to
lay the groundwork for its user, and leading
on to a more advanced or detailed or particu-
larized study, e. g. , T. H. Stevenson, Politics
and Government (Totowa, N. J. : Littlefield,
Adams, 1973).   An outline covers the whole of
its particular subject, but not in detail.   Only
the salient features are emphasized.   Its aim
is not so much to develop understanding (as the
textbook), but to map out an area.   Where a
textbook (or an introduction) is designed for
continuous study, and arranged on the assumption that it will be worked through in sequence,
the outline can also be used quite easily for
reference.   Two examples of outlines are:
G. B. deHuszar and T. H. Stevenson, Political Science, 4th ed. (Totowa, N. J. : Littlefield,
Adams, 1965), and G. A. Jacobsen and M. H.
Lipman, Political Science, new ed. (New York:
Barnes & Noble, 1956).

2.   Conference Proceedings: At times universities and
independent organizations issue the proceedings of
conferences held on important subjects.   An example

of this type of source is A Design for Political
Science: Scope, Objectives, and Methods (Philadelphia: American Academy of Political and Social
Science, 1966). This monograph is actually the
proceedings of a conference held in 1965.

3. Official Publications: This category includes gov-
    ernment documents and the publications of other
    governmental agencies.

4. Professional Literature: From time to time the
    American Political Science Association or other
    regional associations issue publications related to
    the profession. An example of this is P.S., a
    journal devoted to professional activities within the
    field.

5. Research Reports: There are many university
    bureaus and institutes, as well as independent or-
    ganizations, such as the Brookings Institution,
    Rand Corporation and the Center for the Study of
    Democratic Institutions, which issue reports of
    original research on various aspects of political
    science.

6. Reviews of Progress: A source of this kind takes
    the form of a critical summary by a specialist of
    developments in a particular area of political sci-
    ence over a given period. Unfortunately, political
    science has few publications of this type. Perhaps
    the closest we can come is the Political Science
    Annual (Indianapolis: Bobbs-Merrill, 1966+),
    which is really more of a yearbook.

7. Theses and Dissertations: Perhaps the largest
    body of original research is the theses and disser-
    tations produced at colleges and universities each
    year.

8. Unpublished Sources: There are several types of
    unpublished materials that are not theses or dis-
    sertations. They include:
        Notebooks, diaries, memoranda, etc.
        Internal research reports, company files, etc.
        Correspondence, personal files, etc.

B. **Non-Documented Sources:**
> Not least because talking and listening are
> more congenial than reading and writing, such
> sources form a substantial part of the commu-
> nication system of the social sciences and po-
> litical science is no exception.   It is clear
> that they provide something that the other
> sources do not (and perhaps cannot).

1. **Formal:**
    a. Government departments, Federal, State and
        local

    b. Research organizations

    c. Learned and Professional societies

    d. Industry, private and public

    e. Universities and colleges

    f. Consultants

2. **Informal:**
    a. Conversations with colleagues, visitors, etc.

    b. 'Corridor meetings' at conferences, etc.

C. **Reference Sources:**
> It is possible to distinguish a less well-
> defined group of sources, the main function of
> which is to assist the searcher in retrieving
> information from a wide variety of materials.
> Reference sources do not present information
> in a sequence intended to invite continuous
> reading, but are designed to impart separate
> information conveniently arranged for inter-
> mittant consultation.   There is a wide variety
> of reference sources directly or indirectly re-
> lated to political science.

1. **Abstracts:** Abstracts are archetypal secondary
    information sources.   Comprising not merely cita-
    tions but also summaries of the content of publi-
    cations or articles, they manifestly organize the
    primary literature in more convenient form.   As a
    device for the political scientist an abstracting
    service is double-edged: not only does it alert
    him (as an indexing services does) to newly-
    published works that the law of scattering has so

dispersed he would without its aid miss completely, but it can often obviate the actual perusal of the original journals. International Political Science Abstracts (Paris: International Political Science Association, 1951+) is an example of an abstracting service in the field.

2. Bibliographies: In practical terms, a bibliography is an intermediary instrument or device which assists in transmitting recorded information from the producer to the ultimate consumer. It serves to guide the user to desired information in the rather chaotic world of books and other forms of communication. An example of a current bibliography is the International Bibliography of Political Science (Chicago: Aldine Pub. Co. , 1952+). An example of a retrospective bibliography is: Maryland University. Bureau of Governmental Research, Political Science: A Selected Bibliography of Books in Print (College Park, Md. : 1961), edited by Franklin Burdette.

3. Dictionaries: As one of our most common reference sources, the dictionary is probably less in need of explanation than any other. Its concern is words: either the general words of a language, or, as in this case, the special terms of a particular subject discipline. In a field like political science, so dependent by its very nature on communication, there is a need to understand the meaning of terms especially with regard to new and expanding subfields. The most extensive general work of this kind is Joseph Dunner, ed. , Dictionary of Political Science (Totowa, N. J. : Littlefield, Adams, 1970). Many other dictionaries of a more specialized nature are also available, such as Jack C. Plano and Robert E. Riggs, Dictionary of Political Analysis (Hinsdale, Ill. : Dryden Press, 1973).

4. Directories and Biographical Works: Directories are basically lists of names and addresses, arranged for reference purposes in a variety of ways to match the requirements of their users, and frequently updated. For political science, the Biographical Directory (Washington, D. C. : American Political Science Association, 1973) is a member list with biographical data.

5. Encyclopedias: Of all reference sources the encyclopedia is probably the best known, and the student will already be familiar with the form and
function of the great general multi-volume encyclopedias. There is no truly encyclopedic work in
the field of political science generally. Perhaps
the closest we can come is the International Encyclopedia of the Social Sciences (New York: Macmillan, 1963), edited by David Sills. This 15-
volume set covers a great many items related to
political science.

6. Guides to the Literature: Guides to the literature
are not exactly subject bibliographies in the ordi-
nary sense because they usually go beyond the nor-
mal limits of enumerative bibliography in including
not merely lists of references but discussions of
the functions and uses of the various types of
literature. Such a guide normally gives examples
of sources in its chosen field, drawing on all types
of material, and it discusses the sources, evaluates them, and shows how one can compensate for
the deficiencies in another. It can guide the user
to other sources of information not necessarily in
published form, such as specialized libraries, international governmental or non-governmental organizations, and report literature. Two excellent
guides for political science are Clifton Brock's The
Literature of Political Science: A Guide for Students, Librarians and Teachers (New York: R. R.
Bowker, 1969) and Frederick L. Holler's The Information Sources of Political Science, 2d ed. (Santa Barbara, Calif.: ABC-Clio, Inc., 1975). This
latter work is now published in 5 volumes.

7. Handbooks: One of the reference works most frequently consulted by the active political scientist is
the handbook. These compilations offer information on a particular subject in handy form. Although individual reference books of this type vary
considerably in arrangement and format, they bear
a certain resemblance to encyclopedias. A good
example is the Political Handbook and Atlas of the
World (New York: Harper & Row, 1927+).

8. Indexes: For many years, among the most important bibliographical tools for controlling the peri-

odical literature of political science have been
those indexes which have analyzed the contents not
just of one but of a wide range of titles. For political science the most extensive indexing service
is the Social Sciences Index (New York: H. W.
Wilson, 1916+), formerly known as the International Index and more recently the Social Sciences and
Humanities Index. Another important indexing service is the Public Affairs Information Service Bulletin (New York: 1915+). Another less extensive
type is ABC Pol Sci: Advance Bibliography of
Contents: Political Science (Santa Barbara, Calif.:
ABC-Clio Press, 1969+).

9. Yearbooks: A yearbook is an annually published
reference work usually containing statistical data
or a description of factual developments during
specific periods of time. The particular information
which is subject to change or requires frequent up-
dating. There are many types of yearbooks in political science and its various subfields. One of
the better known of these is the Statesman's Yearbook
(New York: St. Martins Press, 1869+).

D. Periodical Sources:
            Of the scholarly journals in the field which
report the findings of original research The
American Political Science Review and The
Journal of Politics are two good examples.
There are, of course, many others. Other
types of periodicals specialize in interpreting
and commenting on developments reported in
the primary literature. The scholarly journal
Foreign Affairs might be considered as one of
these.

Conclusion

Although the bibliographic information retrieval devices

of political science are steadily improving, there are seri-

ous gaps which still exist in the bibliographic control of po-

litical subject matter and the technology of political informa-

tion exchange. Despite many prescriptions concerning bibli-

ographical needs within political science, coming from both

librarians and political scientists themselves, there never has been any empirical analysis of information transfer and needs among political scientists. Additional study with regard to this area would appear to be a prerequisite for the rational design and development of future information retrieval devices in the field.

Chapter Two

GENERAL SELECTION SOURCES
FOR MATERIALS IN POLITICAL SCIENCE

In this era of the information explosion librarians are
faced with a bewildering array of new books, periodicals
and various media on an equally bewildering assortment of
information and promotional literature about these new publications. Most librarians will have to rely upon the various
material selection aids, which represent a coverage of current publishing by many people, reporting their pooled judg-
ment of the best being published.

There exist today many general selection aids which
can assist the average librarian to do a reasonably satis-
factory job. They vary a great deal in terms of coverage,
format, frequency and usefulness. For book materials in
political science the general reviewing media give reasonably
good coverage. Advance notices can be located in the ad-
vertising pages and forecast lists of Publishers Weekly, Library Journal, and Forthcoming Books, or in the blurbs of
individual publishers. After obtaining basic bibliographical
data such as author, title, publisher, date, and price, a
specific title can be checked in Kirkus Reviews, which
carries informal and informative reviews several weeks before publication date. The "Book Review" section of Library
Journal contains signed reviews written by librarians which
indicate usefulness for various types of libraries.

Near the date of publication, a title may appear in the
Weekly Record, which was formerly a part of Publishers
Weekly but is now issued separately. This kind of listing
will appear if the publisher has sent a copy of the book in
advance of the publication date. At approximately the same
time, reviews appear in the weekly book review sections of
such newspapers as the New York Times, Washington Post,
and those of other major metropolitan areas. Most of these
reviewing media present timely reviews either before publication or near the date of publication [Mary D. Carter, Wal-
lace J. Bonk, Rose M. Magrill, Building Library Collections,
4th ed. (Metuchen, N.J.: Scarecrow Press, 1974), pp. 104-
5].

There are a variety of review media which cover materials after they are published. A guide to current books
published by the American Library Association is the Booklist. The Book Review Digest, published by H. W. Wilson
Company, lists new books after a number of reviews have
appeared. General periodicals, such as Atlantic and Har-
pers, have excellent book review sections but are inclined
to review books after publication date [Robert N. Broadus,
Selecting Materials for Libraries (New York: H. W. Wilson,
1973), pp. 61-8; see Chapter Six for an excellent discussion
of book review sources].

There are also selection aids of basic collections,
which can be used to fill gaps and strengthen the political
science collection. The H. W. Wilson Company publishes
a number of these such as The Public Library Catalog, The
High School Catalog, and The Childrens Catalog, all of which
list some political science materials relative to their respective levels. There are several aids to the selection of
books for junior college and liberal arts college libraries.

The most recent college lists are Books for College Libraries (Chicago: American Library Association, 1967), which includes a selected list of books published before 1964, and the American Library Association's current reviewing medium, Choice. Two retrospective basic lists are: (1) Catalog of the Lamont Library (1953), which was intended to support the particular needs of the Harvard undergraduate program, and (2) The Shelf List of the University of Michigan's Undergraduate Library (1958-62). For junior colleges, Frank J. Bertalan's Junior College Library Collection is a useful tool, as is James Pirie's Books for Junior College Libraries [Carter, Bonk, Magrill, Building Library Collections, 4th ed., pp. 106-7].

A librarian charged with building a political science collection for a new college library will have need of retrospective tools, as well as guides to current publishing. Checking the Lamont Library Catalog and the University of Michigan Undergraduate Shelflist as well as Books for College Libraries for materials in political science would provide a broader view of past titles than using any one of them alone. All three were developed with somewhat different aims and consequently complement each other. An excellent older list, Charles B. Shaw's List of Books for College Libraries (1931 and its 1931-38 continuation, 1940) may be used profitably for retrospective purchases. In retrospective acquisition, care must be exercised to avoid selection of obsolete materials.

GENERAL BOOK SELECTION SOURCES*

Guides to Reviews and Selection Sources:
Book Review Digest. New York: H. W. Wilson, 1905+

*See footnote next page.

v. 1+

Includes recent books published in the English language.
Each book is entered under author, with full bibliographic data, followed by a brief descriptive note and some
excerpts. Has an annual cumulation which contains a fair
number of books on and related to political science.

Book Review Index.   Detroit: Gale Research, 1965+
    v. 1+
    Contains reviews from about 200 English-language peri-
    odicals and arranges the citations alphabetically by the
    author of the book reviewed.   Somewhat more extensive
    than the Book Review Digest.   Coverage of materials
    related to political science is good.

Current Reviewing Sources:

Booklist.   Chicago: American Library Association, 1905+
    v. 1+
    Each current issue contains reviews of 100-125 books
    recommended for library purchase.   Reviews are writ-
    ten by specialists and level is indicated.   Inclusion of
    political science titles is not overly extensive.

Choice.   Chicago: Association of College and Research
    Libraries, 1964+   v. 1+
    Reviews of about 600 to 700 titles are provided in each
    issue, for an annual total of over 6000 titles.   Reviews
    are critical and unsigned.   Has good coverage of regular
    monographs and reference works in political science.

Kirkus Reviews.   New York: Kirkus Service, 1933+
    This publication makes available to booksellers, li-
    brarians, and others informal and informative reviews of
    books.   Normally books are reviewed before publication.
    Not extensive in reviewing materials in political science.

Library Journal.   New York: R. R. Bowker, 1876+
    v. 1+
    The book review section has reviews written by li-

---

*Information for the following sections was gathered from
first-hand review of the materials cited as well as from the
Carter, Bonk, Magrill and the Broadus books.   For in-depth
discussions of the selection process these two books are a
must for the librarian.

brarians, giving practical evaluations of current titles.
The reviews are arranged by broad subject areas. Has
fairly good coverage of political science subjects.

New York Times Book Review. New York: New York
   Times, 1896+
   Contains informative reviews, often written by authorities. Covers most of the popular subjects related to
   political science.

Publishers Weekly. New York: R. R. Bowker, 1872+
   v. 1+
   The American book trade journal carries a column
   which reviews forthcoming books, many of which are
   related to political science.

Retrospective Selection Sources:

Library Journal Book Review. New York: R. R. Bowker,
   1967+
   An annual publication of all the reviews that have appeared in Library Journal, arranged by subject and indexed by author and title. Contains a good selection
   of political science books.

Public Library Catalog. New York: W. H. Wilson,
   1934+
   A selected, classified list of over 11,000 nonfiction
   titles which have been suggested by practicing librarians
   because of their usefulness in public library collections.
   Includes a good selection of books and related political
   science materials.

Voigt, Melvin J. Books for College Libraries. Chicago:
   American Library Association, 1967.
   Prepared with the assistance of Joseph H. Treyz this
   work lists 53,410 titles, carefully selected to support
   basic undergraduate studies. Includes titles published
   before 1964. It is arranged by the Library of Congress
   classification scheme, with author and subject indexes.
   Each entry includes author, title, edition, pagination,
   and Library of Congress card number. One may con-
   sider Choice mentioned above as its current continuation.

Bertalan, Frank. Junior College Library Collection.
   1970 ed. Newark, N.J.: Bro-Dart Foundation, 1970.

The current edition is a selected list of more than 22,000 books. Has a good collection of political science materials.

Pirie, James. Books for Junior College Libraries. Chicago: American Library Association, 1969. Lists nearly 20,000 titles and has a wide selection of political science books.

Senior High School Library Catalog. New York: H. W. Wilson, 1926+ Includes materials for grades 10-12. Lists some political science books.

Selected Supplementary Sources:

Bulletin of the Public Affairs Information Service. New York: 1915+ A weekly publication with four cumulations within the year, followed by an annual volume. It is an index to economic, social, and political affairs selected from periodicals, papers, books, government documents, and typewritten and mimeographed materials, published in English throughout the world.

Reference Services Review. Ann Arbor, Mich.: Pierian Press, 1973+ v. 1+ Includes reviews of new reference books, an annotated list of reference books too new to have been reviewed, and an index to reference book reviews.

POLITICAL SCIENCE BOOK SELECTION SOURCES

Reviews of the Literature:

The oldest channel for the selection of books is the book review section of a multipurpose journal. Many of the major journals in political science carry extensive book review sections or bibliographic essays which review several books on a specific topic. The list below includes the leading political science journals containing book review sections.

American Academy of Political and Social Science.

Annals, 1889+; The American Behavioral Scientist, 1957+;
The American Journal of International Law, 1907+; American
Journal of Political Science, 1957+; American Political Science Review, 1906+; British Journal of Political Science,
1971+; Bulletin of the Bibliographic Information Center for
the Study of Political Science, 1972+; Canadian Journal of
Political Science, 1968+; Canadian Public Administration,
1958+; Comparative Political Studies, 1968+; Ethics, 1890+;
Foreign Affairs, 1922+; Government and Opposition, 1965+;
International Affairs, 1922+; The International Lawyer,
1966+; International Organization, 1947+; Journal of Comparative Administration, 1969+; The Journal of Conflict Resolution, 1957+; Journal of International Affairs, 1947+; Journal of Politics, 1939+; Orbis, 1957+; Policy Sciences,
1970+; Policy Studies Journal, 1972+; Political Quarterly,
1930+; Political Science, 1948+; Political Science Quarterly,
1886+; Political Studies, 1953+; Political Theory, 1973+;
Politics, 1966+; Politics and Society, 1970+; Polity, 1968+;
Public Administration, 1922+; Public Administration Review,
1940+; The Public Opinion Quarterly, 1937+; The Review of
Politics, 1939+; Teaching Political Science, 1973+; Urban
Affairs Quarterly, 1965+; Western Political Quarterly,
1948+; World Affairs, 1837+; World Justice, 1959+; World
Politics, 1948+.

Specialized Reviewing Media:

    Harmon, Robert B. Suggestions for a Basic Political Sci-
      ence Library; A Guide to the Building of a Political
      Science Collection for School, Classroom or Individual.
      San Jose, Calif.: Bibliographic Information Center for
      the Study of Political Science, 1970.
      Annotated and classified list of about 100 recommended
      titles.

Perspective.   Washington, D. C. : Operations & Policy
   Research Institution, 1972+   v. 1+   (monthly)
   An international review of books on government, politics and international affairs.   Arrangement is by broad
   subject areas, and there is an author index.

The Political Science Reviewer.   Hampden-Sydney, Va. :
   Intercollegiate Studies Institute, Hampden-Sydney College, 1971+   v. 1+
   Each annual volume covers some 20 titles in 9 or 10
   reviews and critical bibliographic essays, with related
   readings footnoted.
   Contributions are by noted authorities, and an attempt
   is made to accomodate a broad range of political persuasion.   Reviews of textbooks, reprints, and classics,
   as well as current studies.

SELECTION SOURCES FOR NON-BOOK MATERIALS

Libraries have always collected some types of non-book
materials such as pamphlets, maps, periodicals, and clip-
pings.   Currently there has been growing emphasis on such
materials as films, musical and spoken recordings, and
microforms of various kinds.   The political science collection will undoubtedly have a number of these types of materials in it.

General Sources:

Audiovisual Market Place.   New York: R. R. Bowker,
   1969+
   Includes directory information for producers of non-
   print materials, listing under name of producer,
   medium/media produced, and subject.   Also includes
   associations, annotated list of reference publications,
   review services, and other information of interest to
   political scientists.

Multi-Media Reviews Index.   Ann Arbor, Mich. : Pierian
   Press, 1970+
   An annual publication which indexes reviews from a
   number of journals of films, filmstrips, non-classical

records and tapes, and miscellaneous media forms.
Includes a fair number of materials related to political
science.

Films and Filmstrips:

Film Review Index. Monterey Park, Calif.: Audio Visu-
al Associates, 1970+
Issued quarterly this publication cites location of film
reviews in about 75 periodicals. Includes many items
related to political topics.

Jones, Emily S., ed. College Film Library Collection.
Williamsport, Pa.: Bro-Dart, 1972   2v
Includes recommended films for undergraduate use. It
is arranged by subject and each entry is annotated.
Lists some films on political subjects.

Recordings:

Educators' Guide to Free Tapes, Scripts and Transcrip-
tions. Randolph, Wis.: Educators' Progress Service,
1955+
This publication is issued annually and is annotated.
Its purpose is to meet the needs of teachers. Includes
recordings related to political events.

National Center for Audio Tapes. Catalog. Boulder,
Colorado: 1970. Suppl. 1971.
An annotated subject list of available tapes many of
which are suitable for curriculum use in political science.

Microforms:

Guide to Microforms in Print. Washington, D.C.: Micro-
card Editions, 1961-
This work is an annual alphabetical listing of microform
publications offered for sale in the United States.
Many materials relate to political science. Also has a
subject guide which is published separately.

Microform Review. Weston, Conn.: 1972+
Published quarterly this continuation contains critical

and detailed reviews of new microform projects, as
well as reviews of new books and citations to recent
articles on the subject of micropublishing.   Some of
the reviews cover materials related to political topics.

Periodicals:

Farber, Evan I.   Classified List of Periodicals for the
College Library.   5th ed.   Westwood, Mass. :   Faxon,
1972.
Contains detailed annotations of over 1000 periodical
titles (published before 1969) considered important to
be in a liberal arts college library.   Includes the major journals in political science and related sub-fields.

Katz, William.   Magazines for Libraries.   With Berry
Gargal.   2d ed.   New York: R. R. Bowker, 1972.
This work is an annotated bibliography of approximately 4500 periodicals considered suitable for the general
reader.   Comments on the value of each periodical for
a particular type of library.   Lists only the more important journals in political science and law.

Ulrich's International Periodicals Directory.   New York:
R. R. Bowker, 1932+
This massive work is arranged by subject with bibliographic information and some data on circulation, indexing, etc. , to about 50,000 publications issued more
often than once a year.   Has the largest list of political science periodicals.

Pamphlets:

Bulletin of the Public Affairs Information Service.   New
York: Public Affairs Information Service, 1915+
A basic index to information on economic, social and
political affairs selected from periodicals, papers,
books, government documents, and typewritten and
mimeographed materials, published in English throughout the world.   Often includes pamphlet items on political topics.

Vertical File Index.   New York: H. W. Wilson, 1932/34+
Issued monthly, this publication is a subject listing of
new pamphlets, leaflets, etc. , considered to be of

possible interest in school, college, public, and business libraries.   Lists many political science items.

II. SUGGESTIONS FOR THE LIBRARY COLLECTION
IN POLITICAL SCIENCE

<u>General Note</u>

Newspapers, radio, and television are important sources of information, but the person who depends solely on these sources will have an imperfect picture of the world around him. They give only a disconnected story of the sensational --the newsworthy--events. They tell little of the whys and wherefores.

Magazines of general circulation contain useful material, but they do not go deeply into particular questions. Where do you find a law? How do you look up a court decision? Where can you find information on the United Nations? How do you find out how your congressman has voted? What are some good books on the U.S.S.R.? Many aids and services have been designed to make such information readily available.

Important information-dispensing centers are the more than 7500 public libraries and the many hundreds of academic and private libraries that are open to the public. Politics is a field in which a flow of fresh materials is especially important for the library. New issues are brought up and crowd out the older ones. Libraries of all kinds play an increasingly important role in the education of citizens.

This section provides a collection of suggested titles

for the political science collection.   Selection was based on
the reviews contained in the sources listed in Chapter Two
or their repeated citation in the literature.   Each entry includes full bibliographical information along with Library of
Congress classification numbers and card numbers.   Brief
descriptive annotations are also provided for each citation.
Chapter Three covers books and monographs under broad
subject headings.   Chapter Four contains a selected listing
of important reference materials that are arranged by type.
Finally, Chapter Five covers the more prominent periodicals
and journals, listed in alphabetical order.

Chapter Three

BOOKS IN THE FIELD

Books on or related to political science tumble off the
presses each year by the thousands. The problem is to find
out what have been printed, where, and how to get them.
Aids to access to books are library card catalogs, publishers'
and dealers' catalogs, book reviews, and bibliographies such
as the one below.

AFRICA--POLITICS

The Administration of Change in Africa; Essays in the
   Theory and Practice of Development Administration in
   Africa. E. Philip Morgan, editor. New York: Dunellen, 1974. 420p. 70-148704 JQ1875.A5 1974
   Most of these papers were prepared for a symposium
   held at Syracuse University in May, 1970 on development administration in Africa. Includes bibliographical references.

Africa in World Affairs: The Next Thirty Years. Edited
   by Ali A. Mazuri and Hasu H. Patel. New York:
   Third Press, 1973. 265p. 72-80184 DT30.A348
   1973
   A collection of projective essays discussing the role
   of African nations in international politics.

Africa Independent; A Survey of Political Developments.
   New York: Scribner, 1972. 317p. 70-162750
   DT3C.A35
   A developmental approach to political affairs in Afri-
   can political systems. Based on information contained
   in Keesing's Contemporary Archives.

Bretton, Henry L. Power and Politics in Africa. Chicago: Aldine Pub. Co., 1973. 402p. 72-78212
JQ1873 1973.B73
Emphasizes the role of power in politics in African political relations since 1960.

Carter, Gwendolen M. Southern Africa: Prospects for Change. New York: Foreign Policy Association, 1974.
63p. 73-93659 E744.H43 no.219
A brief but concise discussion of the governments of Southern Africa and their prospects for the future.

McKay, Vernon. Africa in World Politics. Westport, Conn.: Greenwood Press, 1974. 468p. 73-11866
DT30.M24 1974
A reprint of the 1963 ed. An interpretative analysis of African politics since 1960.

Maitland-Jones, J. F. Politics in Africa; The Former British Territories. New York: Norton, 1974.
73-20361 JQ1883 1973.M34
Analyzes the political development of the newer African nations.

Rubin, Leslie. Introduction to African Politics: A Continental Approach. With Brian Weinstein. New York: Praeger, 1974. 326p. 79-149969 JQ1872.R8
A broad approach to the political problems of developing African states.

The State of the Nations: Constraints on Development in Independent Africa. Edited by Michael F. Lofchie. Berkeley, University of California Press, 1971. 305p.
75-121191 JQ1873 1971.S7
A group of interpretative essays dwelling on the political and economic issues in African nations.

Touval, Saadia. The Boundary Politics of Independent Africa. Cambridge, Mass.: Harvard University Press, 1972. 334p. 72-79312 DT30.T68
Written under the auspices of the Center for International Affairs, Harvard University, this work deals with the political issues involved in boundary disputes among African states.

ANARCHISM AND ANARCHISTS

Apter, David E. Anarchism Today. With James Joll.
  Garden City, N.Y.: Doubleday, 1971. 237p. 76-152885
  HX828.A65 1971b
  An interpretative collection of essays on the contempo-
  rary role of anarchism in the world.

Carter, April. The Political Theory of Anarchism. New
  York: Harper & Row, 1971. 116p. 73-162289
  HX833.C34 1971b
  This work explores key themes and ideas within anar-
  chism in relation to other traditions of political theory,
  and to contemporary political and social conditions.

Runkle, Gerald. Anarchism, Old and New. New York:
  Delacorte Press, 1972. 330p. 76-39671 HX833.R83
  Discusses the nature and scope of anarchism in its
  developmental aspects.

Suskind, Richard. By Bullet, Bomb, and Dagger; The
  Story of Anarchism. New York: Macmillan, 1971.
  182p. 75-123137 HX828.S97
  A general, historical analysis of anarchism as it has
  developed in political thought and practice.

ARAB COUNTRIES--POLITICS

Malone, Joseph J. The Arab Lands of Western Asia.
  Englewood Cliffs, N.J.: Prentice-Hall, 1973. 269p.
  73-5948 DS62.8.M344
  Focuses on the politics of the Arab nations.

Society and Political Structure in the Arab World. Edited
  by Menaham Milson. New York: Humanities Press,
  1973. 338p. 73-85037 DS62.8.S65 1973
  These articles were originally presented in a series of
  colloquia on society and political structure in the Arab
  world held in the Van Leer Jerusalem Foundation from
  November 1970 to June 1971.

Trevelyan, Humphrey. The Middle East in Revolution.
  Boston: Gambit, 1970. 275p. 70-121353 DS63.1.T74
  1970
  Details the problems of politics in Arab nations.

ARISTOTLE

   The Politics of Aristotle.   One of the classical works of
      political philosophy.   Many editions are available.

ASIA--POLITICS

   Iriye, Akira.   The Cold War in Asia: A Historical Intro-
      duction.   Englewood Cliffs, N. J. :   Prentice-Hall, 1974.
      214p.   73-16200   DS33. 4. U6I74
      A historical survey of Asian participation in foreign
      affairs.

   McAlister, John T. , comp.   Southeast Asia: The Politics
      of National Integration.   New York: Random House,
      1973.   561p.   72-4754   DS518. 1. M2   1973
      A collection of essays dealing with the basic issues in
      the political development of Southeast Asian nations.

   Peritz, René.   Changing Politics of Modern Asia.   New
      York: Van Nostrand, 1973.   138p.   72-7738
      DS35. P455
      A brief and broad discussion of the character and prac-
      tice of politics in Asian nation states.

   Pye, Lucian W.   Southeast Asia's Political Systems.   2d
      ed.   Englewood Cliffs, N. J. :   Prentice-Hall, 1974.
      116p.   73-8755   JQ96. A2P95   1974
      A general analysis of political affairs in the nation
      states of Southeast Asia.

   Rahul, Ram.   Politics of Central Asia.   New York:
      Barnes & Noble Books, 1974.   183p.   74-175851
      DS786. R28   1974
      Evaluates political problems of Central Asian govern-
      ments and discusses their foreign relations.

   Scott, Roger.   The Politics of New States; A General
      Analysis with Case Studies from Eastern Asia.   New
      York: Harper & Row, 1971.   201p.   76-171974
      DS35. S37   1971
      An interpretative essay on the developmental aspects
      of politics in the newer states of Asia.

   Smith, Roger M. , comp.   Southeast Asia; Documents of
      Political Development and Change.   Ithaca: Cornell

University Press, 1974. 608p. 73-14062 DS518. 1. S58
Presents documents of Southeast Asian politics and analyzes the changes that have taken place.

Waddell, J. Robert E. An Introduction to Southeast Asian
Politics. New York: Wiley, 1972. 305p. 73-174900
JQ96. A3 1972
A purposeful look at the key political issues of South-
east Asia's nation states.

AUTHORITY, POLITICAL

Benne, Kenneth D. A Conception of Authority; An Introductory Study. New York: Russell & Russell, 1971.
227p. 75-151538 HM271. B4 1971
A reprint of the 1944 ed. Examines the concept of authority in political affairs and its effect upon nations.

Friedrich, Carl J. Tradition and Authority. New York:
Praeger, 1972. 144p. 74-95674 JC571. F695
Evaluates the traditional aspects of authority and its
relationship to governmental power.

Harvard Tercentenary Conference of Arts and Sciences,
Cambridge, Mass. , 1936. Authority and the Individual.
New York: Arno Press, 1974. 371p. 73-14144
JA36. H3 1936a
Reprint of the 1937 edition. Papers presented at a
symposium discussing the concept of authority in po-
litical matters.

Schwartz, Thomas, comp. Freedom and Authority; An
Introduction to Social and Political Philosophy. Encino,
Calif. : Dickenson Pub. Co. , 1973. 426p. 72-87315
JC571. S386
A collection of essays exploring the role of authority
and freedom in the development of political thought.

Simon, Yves René Marie. A General Theory of Authority.
Westport, Conn. : Greenwood Press, 1973. 167p.
72-9920 HM271. S45 1973
A reprint of the 1962 edition. An interpretative study
which reviews and investigates the relationship of authority and liberty.

BUREAUCRACY

Albrow, Martin. Bureaucracy. New York: Praeger,
1970. 157p. 76-95661 JF1351.H35
A sound and balanced appraisal of bureaucracy in
modern political organizations.

Blau, Peter M. Bureaucracy in Modern Society. With
Marshall W. Meyer. 2d ed. New York: Random
House, 1971. 180p. 73-156338 JF1351.B55 1971
Discusses the role of bureaucracy in government and
its effect upon modern society in general.

Dalby, Michael T. , comp. Bureaucracy in Historical
Perspective. Edited with Michael S. Werthman.
Glenview, Ill. : Scott, Foresman, 1971. 178p.
74-137138 JF1321.D35
Scholarly up-to-date assessments of bureaucracy and
its historical development.

Dvorin, Eugene P. From Amoral to Humane Bureaucracy.
With Robert H. Simmons. San Francisco: Canfield
Press, 1972. 88p. 72-6268 JF1411.D86
Relates the significant aspects of bureaucratic organi-
zation to the structure and functions of governmental
institutions.

Krislov, Samuel. Representative Bureaucracy. Englewood Cliffs, N.J. : Prentice-Hall, 1974. 149p.
73-21814 JF1411.K74
Discusses the role of bureaucracy in representative
government with emphasis on the United States.

Niskanen, William A. Bureaucracy and Representative
Government. Chicago: Aldine, Atherton, 1971. 241p.
77-149841 JF1501.N55
Traces the development of bureaucracy and the organization of representative governmental institutions.

BURKE, EDMUND

Reflections on the Revolution in France. One of the
classics of political philosophy. Several editions are
available.

CAMPAIGN MANAGEMENT

Agranoff, Robert, comp.   The New Style in Election Campaigns.   Boston: Holbrook Press, 1972.   392p.
75-180771   JK2281.A6
Readings on contemporary campaign strategies and
election techniques.

Hershey, Marjorie R.   The Making of Campaign Strategy.
Lexington, Mass. :   Lexington Books, 1974.   164p.
73-21757   JF2112.C3H47
Presents a discussion of basic campaign management
along with the techniques of electioneering.

Herzberg, Donald G.   A Student Guide to Campaign Politics.   With J. W. Peltason.   New York: McGraw-Hill,
1970.   84p.   73-134594   JK2283.H47
An introductory examination of basic campaign techniques and methods.

Rosenbloom, David L.   The Political Marketplace.   New
York: Quadrangle Books, 1972.   948p.   72-77926
JK2283.R64
A directory of election and campaign agencies.

Shadegg, Stephen C.   The New How to Win an Election.
New York: Taplinger Pub. Co. , 1972.   189p.
76-163887   JF2112.C3S53
Covers basic methods involved in conducting a political
campaign.

Simpson, Dick W.   Winning Elections: A Handbook in
Participatory Politics.   Chicago: Swallow Press, 1972.
194p.   78-171874   JK2283.S54
A handbook for electioneering and campaign management.

CHINA--POLITICS AND GOVERNMENT

Barnett, A. Doak.   Uncertain Passage: China's Transi-
tion to the Post-Mao Era.   Washington: Brookings
Institution, 1974.   387p.   73-22482   DS777.55.B333
An analysis of contemporary Chinese political affairs.

Chai, Winberg.   The New Politics of Communist China;
Modernization Process of a Developing Nation.   Pacific

Palisades, Calif. : Goodyear Pub. Co. , 1972.   305p.
78-188277   DS777. 55. C334
A critical look at modern politics on mainland China.

China and the Great Powers: Relation with the United
States, the Soviet Union, and Japan.   Edited by Francis
O. Wilcox.   New York: Praeger, 1974.   103p.
74-1736   DS740. 4. C354525
A group of essays on Chinese foreign relations with
major world powers.

Hinton, Harold C.   An Introduction to Chinese Politics.
New York: Praeger, 1973.   323p.   72-75682
DS777. 55. H5514
An influential assessment of China's politics, both
communist and nationalist.

Ideology and Politics in Contemporary China.   Edited by
Chalmers Johnson.   Seattle: University of Washington
Press, 1973.   390p.   72-11514 DS777. 55. I3
A collection of essays based on papers from the 5th
conference sponsored by the American Council of
Learned Societies and the Social Science Research
Council.

Liu, James T. C. , comp.   Political Institutions in Traditional China: Major Issues.   New York: Wiley,
1974.   156p.   74-1242 DS740. L55
This collection of essays covers the major issues of
China's government.

North, Robert C.   The Foreign Relations of China.   2d
ed.   Encino, Calif. : Dickenson Pub. Co. , 1974.
172p.   73-87461 DS740. 4. N58   1974
An interpretative study of China's foreign affairs by
an expert.

Pye, Lucian W.   China: An Introduction.   Boston: Little,
Brown, 1972.   384p.   72-187711 DS706. P9
An important general study on all phases of modern
China's development.

Starr, John B.   Ideology and Culture; An Introduction to
the Dialectic of Contemporary Chinese Politics.   New
York: Harper & Row, 1973.   300p.   72-12471
JQ1503 1973. S7
A provocative analysis of China's politics.

Townsend, James R. Politics in China. Boston: Little,
Brown, 1974.   377p.   73-11962 JQ1503 1974. T67
1974
Traces the development of Chinese politics since 1949.

Whyte, Martin K. Small Groups and Political Rituals in
China. Berkeley: University of California Press,
1974.   271p.   73-80822 HX388. 5. W47
Discusses communist self-criticism tactics and pre-
sents case studies on small groups within Communist
China's politics.

CIVIL RIGHTS

Abernathy, Mabra G. Civil Liberties Under the Constitution. 2d ed. New York: Dodd, Mead, 1972.   623p.
78-38566 KF4748. A2   1972
A critical and comprehensive review of the issue of
civil rights in the United States.

Abraham, Henry J. Freedom and the Court; Civil Rights
and Liberties in the United States. 2d ed. New York:
Oxford University Press, 1972.   397p.   75-177991
KF4749. A73   1972
Analyzes the problem of civil rights and liberties as
handled by the Supreme Court.

Caster, Jonathan D. The Politics of Civil Liberties.
New York: Harper & Row, 1972.   322p.   72-82899
KF4749. C33
Discusses the role of politics in U.S. civil rights
issues from a behavioral point of view.

Duchacek, Ivo D. Rights & Liberties in the World Today;
Constitutional Promise & Reality. Santa Barbara,
Calif.: ABC-Clio, 1973.   269p.   72-95263 JC571. D86
1973
An international comparison of civil rights in various
nations.

Wolfe, Alan. The Seamy Side of Democracy: Repression
in America. New York: D. McKay Co. , 1973.
306p.   72-96707 JC599. U5W64
A detailed survey of violence in U.S. civil rights en-
counters.

COMMUNISM

Childs, David. Marx and the Marxists; An Outline of
Practice and Theory. New York: Barnes & Noble,
1973. 367p. 73-186254 HX36.C52 1973
Explores the historical development of Communism and
Socialism.

Cohen, Carl, ed. Communism, Fascism, and Democracy;
The Theoretical Foundations. 2d ed. New York:
Random House, 1972. 643p. 70-161455 JC348.C63
1972
Introduces some of the diverse concepts and theories
in the ideologies of Communism, Fascism and Democracy.

Cohen, Lenard J., comp. Communist Systems in Comparative Perspective. Edited with Jane P. Shapiro.
Garden City, N.Y.: Anchor Press, 1974. 530p.
73-81456 JC474.C624
A group of comparative studies on various communist
regimes.

Comparative Communist Political Leadership. By Carl
Beck and others. New York: D. McKay Co., 1973.
319p. 72-75454 HX44.C647
Shows how leadership is applied in a variety of communist governments.

Ebenstein, William. Today's Isms; Communism, Fas-
cism, Capitalism, Socialism. 7th ed. Englewood
Cliffs, N.J.: Prentice-Hall, 1973. 266p. 72-13699
HN18.E2 1973
A basic introduction to modern political and economic
ideologies.

Ellis, Harry B. Ideals and Ideologies: Communism,
Socialism, and Capitalism. New, rev. print. New
York: World Pub., 1973. 255p. 70-155079
HX40.E5 1973
A broad survey of leading political ideologies.

Hyde, Douglas A. Communism Today. Notre Dame, Ind.:
University of Notre Dame Press, 1973. 173p.
72-12639 HX40.H88 1973
Analyzed the origins and development of Communism
as applied in modern communist states.

Prpic, George J.   A Century of World Communism; A
   Selective Chronological Outline.   Woodbury, N.Y.:
   Barron's Educational Series, 1974.   322p.   74-166318
   HX36.P76   1974
   Outlines the historical development of Communism.

COMPARATIVE GOVERNMENT

Anderson, Charles W.   Issues of Political Development.
   With F. R. von der Mehden and C. Young.   2d ed.
   Englewood Cliffs, N.J.: Prentice-Hall, 1974.   278p.
   73-13963   JF60.A53   1974
   Discusses the comparative development of new states
   and political problems.

Beer, Samuel H.   Modern Political Development.   New
   York: Random House, 1974.   141p.   73-20358
   JF31.B42
   Traces consitutional history in various national govern-
   ments and focuses on economic developments in modern
   states.

Bill, James A.   Comparative Politics; The Quest for
   Theory.   With Robert L. Hardgrave, Jr.   Columbus,
   Ohio: Merrill, 1973.   261p.   72-92139   JF51.B53
   A theoretical analysis of comparative politics.

Blondel, Jean.   Comparing Political Systems.   New York:
   Praeger, 1972.   260p.   72-88041   JF51.B562
   Attempts to classify world wide political systems and
   applies an analytical framework to understand their
   activities.

Browne, Eric C.   Coalition Theories: A Logical and Empirical Critique.   Beverly Hills, Calif.: Sage Publications, 1973.   95p.   73-84900   JF331.B76
   Discusses the relationship of coalition governments and
   cabinet systems.

Carter, Gwendolen M.   Major Foreign Powers.   With
   John H. Herz.   6th ed.   New York: Harcourt Brace
   Jovanovich, 1972.   743p.   78-179411   JF51.C3   1972
   A textbook in comparative government, which covers
   the political systems of Great Britain, France,
   Germany and the Soviet Union.

Comparative Politics Today; A World View. General editor: Gabriel A. Almond. Boston: Little, Brown,
 1974. 477p. 73-17788 JF51. C62
 Experts from a number of areas provide a collection of
 interpretative essays on comparative political systems.

Cord, Robert L. Political Science: An Introduction.
 With J. A. Medeiros and W. S. Jones. New York:
 Appleton-Century-Crofts, 1974. 673p. 73-13577
 JF51. C63
 A general survey of comparative government and politi-
 cal science.

Dragnich, Alex N. Major European Governments. With
 Jorgen Rasmussen. 4th ed. Homewood, Ill. : Dorsey
 Press, 1974. 524p. 73-91793 JN12. D7 1974
 A basic text and survey of leading European govern-
 ments and other political institutions.

Eisenstadt, Shmuel N. Building States and Nations. Edited with Stein Rokhan. Beverly Hills, Calif. : Sage
 Publications, 1973+ v. 1+ 73-77873 JF11. E47
 A series of volumes on comparative government and
 politics edited by two leading authorities.

Friedrich, Carl J. Limited Government: A Comparison.
 Englewood Cliffs, N. J. : Prentice-Hall, 1974. 139p.
 74-802 JF51. F723
 A comparative analysis of constitutional history and the
 concept of limited government.

Irish, Marian D. An Introduction to Comparative Politics;
 Twelve Nation States. With Elke Frank. New York:
 Appleton-Century-Crofts, 1972. 427p. 70-184714
 JF51. I7
 A general survey of 12 nations examining their various
 functional units of government.

Johnson, Samuel A. Essentials of Comparative Government. Revised. Woodbury, N. Y. : Barron's Educational Series, 1973. 210p. 74-167276 JF51. J6 1973
 An introductory survey covering the different aspects
 of the field.

La Palombara, Joseph G. Politics Within Nations. Englewood Cliffs, N. J. : Prentice-Hall, 1974. 625p.
 74-3081 JF51. L36

An in-depth treatise on comparative government focusing on political participation.

CONSERVATISM, POLITICAL ASPECTS

Brudnoy, David, comp.   The Conservative Alternative.
Minneapolis: Winston Press, 1973.   274p.   73-76153
JA84. U5B75
A collection of essays providing a general introduction
to conservatism as a political concept.

Meyer, Frank S. , ed.   What Is Conservatism?   New
York: Holt, Rinehart and Winston, 1964.   242p.
64-11014   JK271. M44
Introduces some of the diverse views associated with
this concept.

Turner, William W.   Power in the Right.   Berkeley,
Calif. :   Ramparts Press, 1971.   272p.   72-158916
E839. 5. T85
Considers the conservative approach in U. S. politics
and government.

CORRUPTION (IN POLITICS)

Cook, Fred J.   American Political Bosses and Machines.
New York: F. Watts, 1973.   153p.   73-6777
JS401. C66
Develops the role of political bosses and machines in
the American political process.   Covers mainly cor-
rupt practices.

Peters, Charles, comp.   Blowing the Whistle; Dissent in
the Public Interest.   Edited with Taylor Branch.   New
York: Praeger, 1972.   305p.   72-185768   JK271. P44
A group of essays covering corrupt practices in American politics in general and executive departments in
particular.

Scott, James C.   Comparative Political Corruption.
Englewood Cliffs, N. J. :   Prentice-Hall, 1972.   166p.
75-161461   JF1081. S35
A comparative approach to corruption in politics.

DEMOCRATIC PARTY

> Chambers, William N.   The Democrats in American Poli-
> tics; A Short History of a Popular Party.   2d ed.   New
> York: D. Van Nostrand Co. , 1972.   206p.   72-2351
> JK2316. C47   1972
> A popular history of the Democratic Party in American
> politics.

> Davis, Lanny J.   The Emerging Democratic Majority:
> Lessons and Legacies from the New Politics.   New
> York: Stein and Day, 1974.   276p.   73-82142   JK2317
> 1974. D38
> Assesses the role of the Democratic party in U. S. poli-
> tics and government.

> Domhoff, G. W.   Fat Cats and Democrats; The Role of
> the Big Rich in the Party of the Common Man.   Engle-
> wood Cliffs, N. J. : Prentice-Hall, 1972.   203p.
> 78-38791   JK2317 1972. D64
> Covers campaign funds and the role of elites in the
> Democratic party.

> Harris, Fred R.   Now Is the Time; A New Populist Call
> to Action.   New York: McGraw-Hill, 1971.   238p.
> 70-150778   JK2317 1971. H3
> Expounds the general philosophy of the Democratic
> Party on social and economic policies in American pol-
> itics.

> Stewart, John G.   One Last Chance; The Democratic
> Party, 1974-76.   New York: Praeger, 1974.   208p.
> 73-3678   JK2317 1974. S8
> A critical appraisal of the Democratic Party and its
> chances for success in contemporary American politics.

DEMOCRACY

> Allman, Joe, comp.   Evaluating Democracy; An Introduc-
> tion to Political Science.   With Walt Anderson.   Paci-
> fic Palisades, Calif. : Goodyear Pub. Co. , 1974.
> 339p.   73-88138   JC423. A514
> A collection of essays which evaluates the role of demo-
> cratic institutions in modern government and politics.

Budge, Ian.   Agreement and the Stability of Democracy.
Chicago: Markham Pub. Co. , 1970.   225p.   72-91018
JC423. B864
Covers the broad sweep of democratic theory as applied
to British politics.

Chabe, Alexander M.   Democracy and Communism.   West-
chester, Ill. : Benefic Press, 1973.   160p.   71-186624
JC433. C43
Examines the origins, development, and ideology of
American Democracy and Marxian Communism and com-
pares their influence on life in the United States and
Russia.

Cohen, Carl.   Democracy.   Athens: University of Georgia
Press, 1971.   302p.   77-142911   JC423. C647
Develops a conceptual framework for analyzing democ-
racy in the contemporary sphere.

Dahl, Robert A.   Size and Democracy.   With Edward T.
Tufte.   Stanford, Calif. : Stanford University Press,
1973.   148p.   72-97200   JC364. D33
Relates the size of states to democratic governmental
structures.

Finley, Moses I.   Democracy Ancient and Modern.   New
Brunswick, N. J. : Rutgers University Press, 1973.
118p.   73-1814   JC79. A8F5
A comparison of ancient and modern democratic theory
and practice.

MacPherson, Crawford B.   Democratic Theory: Essays
in Retrieval.   Oxford: Clarendon Press, 1973.   255p.
73-157532   JC423. M159
This collection of interpretative essays illuminates the
problems and applications of democratic theory.

DIPLOMACY

Clark, Eric.   Diplomat; The World of International Diplomacy.   New York: Taplinger Pub. Co. , 1974.   276p.
73-19076   JX1662. C49   1974
An insight into the diplomatic function in international
negotiation.

Harmon, Robert B.   The Art and Practice of Diplomacy:
   A Selected and Annotated Guide.   Metuchen, N.J.:
   Scarecrow Press, 1971.   355p.   75-142234   JX1662.H273
   Provides background information on all aspects of the
   subject along with an extensive annotated bibliography.

Kertesz, Stephen D., ed.   Diplomacy in a Changing World.
   Edited with M. A. Fitzsimons.   Westport, Conn.:
   Greenwood Press, 1974.   407p.   74-2587   JX1662.K4
   1974
   A reprint of the 1959 ed.   A basic discussion of modern
   diplomatic methods.

Nicolson, Sir Harold George.   Diplomacy.   3d ed. re-
   printed with a new introduction by Lord Butler.   New
   York: Oxford University Press, 1969.   150p.
   71-480725   JX1662.N5   1969
   Considered a classic, this work outlines a history and
   definition of diplomacy.

ELECTIONS

Adamany, David W.   Campaign Finance in America.
   North Scituate, Mass.:   Duxbury Press, 1972.   274p.
   72-77743   JK1991.A627
   Clearly explains the importance of campaign finance in
   U.S. elections.

Alexander, Herbert E.   Political Financing.   Minneapolis:
   Burgess Pub. Co., 1972.   60p.   72-88748   JK1991.A714
   A brief study of campaign financing in U.S. politics
   and elections.

Beech, Linda.   On the Campaign Trail; The Story of Elections.   New York: J. Messner, 1971.   96p.   76-157700
   JK1978.B44
   Using New York Lindsay's 1968 re-election campaign as
   an example, explains how a candidate is nominated,
   raises money, and expresses his views on different
   issues.

Bone, Hugh A.   Politics and Voters.   With Austin Ranney.
   3d ed.   New York: McGraw-Hill, 1971.   149p.
   71-141295   JK1976.B6   1971
   Scholarly assessment of elections and voting in American politics.

Dunn, Delmer D. Financing Presidential Campaigns.
Washington: Brookings Institution, 1972. 168p. 72-64
JK1991. D85
Focuses on the financial aspects of presidential cam-
paigns.

Rose, Richard. Electoral Behavior; A Comparative Handbook. New York: Free Press, 1974. 753p. 72-11285
JF2011. R58
Scholarly, up-to-date assessments of elections and political parties in various nations.

EQUALITY, POLITICAL

Bedau, Hugo A., comp. Justice and Equality. Englewood Cliffs, N.J.: Prentice-Hall, 1971. 185p.
76-140685 JC571. B43
A collection of provocative essays appraising the issue
of equality in the legal sphere.

Rees, John. Equality. New York: Praeger, 1971.
152p. 79-100922 JC575. R44
Explores the concept of equality in the history of political thought.

EUROPE--POLITICS

Albinski, Henry S., comp. European Political Processes;
Essays and Readings. Edited with Lawrence K. Pettit.
2d ed. Boston: Allyn and Bacon, 1974. 538p.
73-85329 JF51. A55 1974
A collection of basic readings covering the activities
of European political institutions and parties.

Beer, Samuel H., ed. Patterns of Government; The Major Political Systems of Europe. Edited with Adam B.
Ulam. 3d ed. New York: Random House, 1973.
778p. 72-681 JN12. B4 1973
A collection of essays by eminent authors on the various European political systems.

European Security and the Atlantic System. Edited by
William T. R. Fox and Warner R. Schilling. New
York: Columbia University Press, 1973. 276p.
72-4248 D1053. E89

A group of essays on European politics from a symposium sponsored by the Institute of War and Peace Studies of Columbia University.

Politics in Europe; Structures and Processes in Some Post-Industrial Democracies.   Edited by Martin O. Heisler.   New York: McKay, 1974.   415p.   72-96709 JN94. A3   1974
Essays focus on the structural and procedural aspects of modern European governments.

Schwartz, Harry.   Eastern Europe in the Soviet Shadow. New York: J. Day Co. , 1973.   117p.   72-2409 DR48. 5. S384
A brief study of politics in the Eastern European nations.   Focuses on Soviet influences.

Smith, Gordon.   Politics in Western Europe;   A Comparative Analysis.   New York: Holmes & Meier Publishers, 1973.   403p.   73-75192   JN94. A5S63   1973
A critical and comparative analysis of Western European politics.

Staar, Richard F.   The Communist Regimes in Eastern Europe.   2d rev. ed.   Stanford, Calif. :   Hoover Institution on War, Revolution, and Peace, 1971.   304p. 70-148364   DR48. 5. S74   1971
Details the role of Communism in the governments of Eastern Europe.

EXECUTIVE POWER

Binkley, Wilfred E.   The Powers of the President; Problems of American Democracy.   New York: Russell & Russell, 1973.   332p.   72-90564   JK516. B5   1973
A reprint of the 1937 ed.   Develops the role of executive power in U. S. politics and government.

Davis, James W.   The National Executive Branch; An Introduction.   New York: Free Press, 1970.   228p. 72-96834   JK421. D37
A preliminary assessment of the executive branch in American politics.

Hirschfield, Robert S. , comp.   The Power of the Presidency; Concepts and Controversy.   2d ed.   Chicago:

Aldine Pub. Co. , 1973.   395p.   71-169513   JK516. H5
1973
A critical analysis of executive power in the United
States.

Johnson, Gerald W.   The Cabinet.   Illustrated by Leonard
E. Fisher.   New York: W. Morrow, 1966.   160p.
66-14362   JK611. J6
Written on the juvenile level; discusses the cabinet in
the executive branch of the U. S. government.

Liston, Robert A.   Presidential Power; How Much Is Too
Much?   New York: McGraw-Hill, 1971.   160p.
70-169021   JK516-L55
A frank discussion of the scope and limits of executive
power.

Strum, Philippa.   Presidential Power and American Democracy.   Pacific Palisades, Calif. : Goodyear Pub.
Co. , 1972.   132p.   75-173791   JK516. S77
Evaluates the problems of executive power in the ef-
fective function of American politics.

FASCISM

Ebenstein, William.   Fascist Italy.   New York: Russell
& Russell, 1973.   310p.   72-84985   DG571. E27   1973
Traces fascist thought as it was incorporated in Italian
politics and government from 1914 to 1945.   First
published in 1934 and again in 1939.

Gregor, A. J.   The Fascist Persuasion in Radical Politics.   Princeton, N. J. : Princeton University Press,
1974.   472p.   73-2463   JC481. G686
Discusses the relationship of Fascism, radicalism and
socialism.

_____.   Interpretations of Fascism.   Morristown, N. J.:
General Learning Press, 1974.   281p.   74-75727
JC481. G692
Using Fascist Italy as a model the author discusses
varying approaches to Fascist thought and practice.

Hamilton, Alistair.   The Appeal of Fascism: A Study of
Intellectuals and Fascism, 1919-1945.   New York:
Macmillan, 1971.   312p.   74-134511   D726. 5. H3   1971b

A study of intellectuals and the influence of Fascist
thought in Europe for the period covered.

Hayes, Paul M. Fascism. New York: Free Press,
1973. 260p. 73-13448 JC481.H37
Examines the foundations of modern Fascism and its
effect on political thought.

Lubasz, Heinz. Fascism: Three Major Regimes. New
York: J. Wiley, 1973. 188p. 72-8902 D726.5.L8
A collection of interpretative essays covering Fascism
in Italy, Germany and Japan.

Schüddekopf, Otto E. Fascism. New York: Praeger
Publishers, 1973. 224p. 72-93189 D726.5.S38 1973
Develops a basic history of Fascist thought.

Tannenbaum, Edward R. The Fascist Experience; Italian
Society and Culture, 1922-1945. New York: Basic
Books, 1972. 357p. 72-76904 DG450.T36
A critical and comprehensive view of Italian Fascism.

FEDERAL GOVERNMENT

Bernier, Ivan. International Legal Aspects of Federalism.
Hamden, Conn.: Archon Books, 1973. 308p. 73-2713
JX4005.B45 1973
Discusses the legal aspects of Federal government in
the international arena.

Derthick, Martha. Between State and Nation; Regional Organizations of the United States. With the assistance
of Gary Bombardier. Washington: Brookings Institution, 1974. 242p. 74-727 JK325.D46
Presents case studies on state and national government
along with emphasis on regional planning.

Elazar, Daniel J. American Federalism; A View from
the States. 2d ed. New York: Crowell, 1972. 256p.
78-165371 JK325.E39 1972
Emphasizes the relationships of national and state
government from the latter's viewpoint.

Feld, Richard D., comp. The Uneasy Partnership: The
Dynamics of Federal, State, and Urban Relations.
Edited with Carl Grafton. Palo Alto, Calif.: National

Press Books, 1973. 322p. 72-97844 JK421.F44
A group of essays assessing urban relationships in comparative federalism in the United States.

Friedrich, Carl J. Trends of Federalism in Theory and Practice. New York: Praeger, 1968. 193p. 68-23352 JC355.F73
Case studies discussing the theoretical aspects of federalism.

Haider, Donald H. When Governments Come to Washington: Governors, Mayors, and Intergovernmental Lobbying. New York: Free Press, 1974. 336p. 73-17643 JK325.H24
Provides a view of state and local officials as they attempt to influence national politics.

Holloway, William V. Intergovernmental Relations in the United States. New York: MSS Information Corp., 182p. 72-7472 JK325.H64
A basic study of American federalism.

Macmahon, Arthur W. Administering Federalism in a Democracy. New York: Oxford University Press, 1972. 196p. 72-177993 JK331.M23
Examines the factors determining the nature of administration in U.S. federalism.

GEOGRAPHY, POLITICAL

Cohen, Saul B. Geography and Politics in a World Divided. 2d ed. New York: Oxford University Press, 1973. 334p. 73-77923 JC319.C58 1973
Details the basic influence of geography on world politics.

De Blij, Harm J. Systematic Political Geography. 2d ed. New York: Wiley, 1973. 485p. 73-5665 JC319.D4 1973
Develops a framework for the understanding of geopolitics.

Gottmann, Jean. The Significance of Territory. Charlottesville: University Press of Virginia, 1973. 169p. 72-87807 JC319.G66
Considers the territorial aspects of global power and politics.

Jackson, William A. D.   A Geography of Politics.   With
   Edward F. Bergman.   Dubuque, Iowa: W. C. Brown,
   1973. 92p.   72-77608   JC319.J19
   A brief discussion of the basic principles of geopolitics.

Pounds, Norman J. G.   Political Geography.   2d ed.
   New York: McGraw-Hill, 1972.   453p.   71-74625
   G121.P6   1972
   A general exploration and analysis of world politics as
   influenced by geographical factors.

GOVERNMENT, PRIMITIVE

Balandier, Georges.   Political Anthropology.   Translated
   from the French by A. M. Sheridan Smith.   New York:
   Vintage Books, 1972.   214p.   72-766   GN490.B3413
   1972
   A general survey and analysis of primitive governmental structures.

Political Anthropology.   Edited by Marc J. Swartz, Victor
   W. Turner and Arthur Tuden.   Chicago: Aldine Pub.
   Co. , 1966.   309p.   66-15210   GN490.P6
   Papers contributed for presentation at the 1964 Annual
   General Meeting of the American Anthropological Asso-
   ciation.

GREAT BRITAIN--POLITICS AND GOVERNMENT

Beer, Samuel H.   The British Political System.   New
   York: Random House, 1974.   243p.   73-21759
   JN175.B43
   Provides a basic discussion of current British politics.

Brennan, Tom.   Politics and Government in Britain; An
   Introductory Survey.   London: Cambridge University
   Press, 1972.   332p.   78-171673   JN231.B685
   A preliminary assessment of the British political pro-
   cess.

Moodie, Graeme C.   The Government of Great Britain.
   3d ed.   New York: Crowell, 1971.   241p.   75-136038
   JN318.M65   1971
   A general exploration of British politics and government basically since 1945.

Punnett, Robert M.   British Government and Politics.   2d
ed.   New York: Norton, 1971.   514p.   71-172525
JN234. 1971. P82
An extensive introductory survey of British politics
since the conclusion of the Second World War.

Rose, Richard.   Politics in England; An Interpretation.
2d ed.   Boston: Little, Brown, 1974.   448p.   73-20921
JN234 1974. R6   1974
An in-depth survey of British political institutions.

Verney, Douglas V.   British Government and Politics;
Life Without a Declaration of Independence.   2d ed.
New York: Harper & Row, 1971.   234p.   70-127333
JN118. V4   1971
A general analysis of politics in Britain.

HOBBES, THOMAS

Leviathan.   One of the classics of political philosophy.
There are numerous editions available.

IMPERIALISM

Cohen, Benjamin J.   The Question of Imperialism; The
Political Economy of Dominance and Dependence.   New
York: Basic Books, 1973.   280p.   73-81036
JC359. C63
Examines the development of economic imperialism in
world affairs.

Curtin, Philip D.   Imperialism.   New York: Walker,
1972.   344p.   75-142853   JC359. C85   1972
A collection of important essays covering imperialism,
colonialism and race discrimination in western civiliza-
tion.

Lichtheim, George.   Imperialism.   New York: Praeger,
1971.   183p.   70-117474   JC359. L53
A rather theoretical development of applied imperialism.

Moon, Parker T.   Imperialism and World Politics.   With
a new introduction by Berenice A. Carroll.   New York:
Garland Pub. , 1973.   583p.   75-147502   JC359. M6
1973

A reprint of the 1926 classic treatise on imperialism and world affairs.

Snyder, Louis L., ed.   The Imperialism Reader; Documents and Readings on Modern Expansionism.   Port Washington, N.Y.: Kennikat Press, 1973.   619p. 72-85293   JC359.S65   1973
A reprint of the 1962 ed.   A group of interpretative essays with documents.

Winslow, Earle M.   The Pattern of Imperialism; A Study in the Theories of Power.   New York: Octagon Books, 1972.   278p.   78-159238   JC359.W55   1972
A reprint of the 1948 ed.   Discusses the development of imperialism in international relations.

INTERNATIONAL LAW

Akehurst, Michael B.   A Modern Introduction to International Law.   New York: Atherton Press, 1970.   367p. 78-22986   JX1308.A43
A balanced appraisal of the problems of modern international law.

Brownlie, Ian.   Principles of Public International Law. 2d ed.   Oxford: Clarendon Press, 1973.   733p. 73-160657   JX3225.B78   1973
A basic introduction to international legal principles.

Corbett, Percy E.   The Growth of World Law.   Princeton, N.J.: Princeton University Press, 1971.   216p. 70-132236   JX3110.C6G76
Clearly explains the role of agencies in international law.

Deming, Richard.   Man and the World: International Law at Work.   New York: Hawthorn Books, 1974.   190p. 73-374   JX3110.D42M35
A general study of the functions of law in the international sphere.

Kirkemo, Ronald B.   An Introduction to International Law. Chicago: Nelson-Hall, 1974.   235p.   73-81677 JX3091.K55
A basic introductory survey on the foundations of the international legal system.

Mann, Fritz A. Studies in International Law. Oxford:
Clarendon Press, 1973. 717p. 73-161528 JX68.M28
A collection of essays covering most of the aspects of
international law.

Schwarzenberger, Georg. International Law and Order.
New York: Praeger, 1971. 298p. 70-161208
JX3275.S314
A classic survey of international legal principles.

Summers, Lionel M. The International Law of Peace.
Dobbs Ferry, N.Y.: Oceana Publications, 1972. 262p.
72-4367 JX3180.S77157
Emphasizes the peaceful aspects of international law.

INTERNATIONAL ORGANIZATION

Claude, Inis L. Swords into Plowshares; The Problems
and Progress of International Organization. 4th ed.
New York: Random House, 1971. 514p. 70-122480
JX1954.C54 1971
In-depth survey of contemporary international organiza-
tions and their historical development.

Goodrich, Leland M., comp. International Organization:
Politics & Process. Edited with David A. Kay. Madison, Wis.: University of Wisconsin Press, 1973.
465p. 72-7986 JX1954.G618
A collection of scholarly readings exploring the political development of international organization.

Jacob, Philip E. The Dynamics of International Organization. With A. L. Atherton, and R. M. Wallenstein.
Rev. ed. Homewood, Ill.: Dorsey Press, 1972.
759p. 76-168299 JX1954.J22 1972
This comprehensive study combines a general survey
of international organization with a specific emphasis
on the United Nations.

Miller, Lynn H. Organizing Mankind: An Analysis of
Contemporary International Organization. Boston:
Holbrook Press, 1972. 365p. 78-172863 JX1954.M494
Traces the development of attempts to organize nations
on the international level. Specifically covers the
United Nations.

Wood, Robert S. , comp. The Process of International
Organization. New York: Random House, 1971.
525p. 79-134018 JX1954. W635
A group of important readings on the growth and development of contemporary international organizations.

INTERNATIONAL RELATIONS

Bobrow, Davis B. International Relations: New Approaches. New York: Free Press, 1972. 95p.
72-77282 JX1291. B63
Explores various approaches to international relations
and suggests new and more fruitful ones.

Coplin, William D. Introduction to International Politics;
A Theoretical Overview. Chicago: Markham Pub. Co. ,
1971. 391p. 72-136616 JX1308. C66
Develops a conceptual framework for analyzing international relations.

Haas, Michael. International Systems; A Behavioral Approach. New York: Chandler Pub. Co. , 1974. 433p.
78-171070 JX1291. H33
Develops the behavioral approach to research in international politics.

Lentner, Howard H. Foreign Policy Analysis; A Comparative and Conceptual Approach. Columbus, Ohio: Merrill, 1973. 295p. 73-85554 JX1291. L45
Discusses the conceptual process of foreign policy making.

Lerche, Charles O. Concepts of International Politics.
With Abdul A. Said. 2d ed. Englewood Cliffs, N. J. :
Prentice-Hall, 1970. 297p. 76-86518 JX1308. L4
1970
Examines and explains the different concepts applicable
to international affairs.

Levi, Werner. International Politics: Foundations of the
System. Minneapolis: University of Minnesota Press,
1974. 285p. 73-84786 JX1391. L43
An outstanding introductory work on international relations and law.

Lieber, Robert J.   Theory and World Politics.   Cam-
    bridge, Mass.: Winthrop, 1972.   166p.   72-185516
    JX1291.L54
    Assesses the theoretical constructs involved in research
    on international affairs.

McGowan, Patrick J.   The Comparative Study of Foreign
    Policy; A Survey of Scientific Findings.   With Howard
    B. Shapiro.   Beverly Hills, Calif.: Sage Publications,
    1973.   256p.   72-98040   JX1291.M282
    A report on various research findings on topics related
    to international relations.

McLellan, David S., comp.   The Theory and Practice of
    International Relations.   With William C. Olson and
    Fred A. Sondermann.   4th ed.   Englewood Cliffs, N.J.:
    Prentice-Hall, 1974.   492p.   74-1249   JX1395.M16
    1974
    A basic reader in the field.

Macridis, Roy C., ed.   Foreign Policy in World Politics.
    4th ed.   Englewood Cliffs, N.J.: Prentice-Hall, 1972.
    428p.   77-172678   JX1391.M32   1972
    A collection of outstanding contributions to the foreign
    relations of major world powers.

Morgenthau, Hans J.   Politics Among Nations; The Strug-
    gle for Power and Peace.   5th ed.   New York: Knopf,
    1973.   617p.   72-328   JX1391.M6   1973
    A general survey of international politics emphasizing
    the role of power relations.

Russett, Bruce M.   Power and Community in World Poli-
    tics.   San Francisco: W. H. Freeman, 1974.   372p.
    73-13590   JX1391.R87
    A power approach to the study of international rela-
    tions.

Sheikh, Ahmed.   International Law and National Behavior;
    A Behavioral Interpretation of Contemporary Interna-
    tional Law and Politics.   New York: Wiley, 1974.
    352p.   73-19922   JX1395.S44
    An introduction to international behavior and law with
    implications for international relations generally.

Sterling, Richard W.   Macropolitics: International Rela-
    tions in a Global Society.   New York: Knopf, 1974.

648p.   73-21769   JX1395. S76   1974
A general survey of international relations.

JUDICIAL PROCESS

Eisenstein, James.   Politics and the Legal Process.
New York: Harper & Row, 1973.   356p.   73-2704
KF380. E35
Evaluates the role of politics in the judicial process in
the United States.

Introduction to Law and the Legal Process.   By Bernard
F. Cataldo and others.   2d ed.   New York: Wiley,
1973.   640p.   72-10666   KF380. I58   1973
An introductory collection of studies on the U. S. legal
system.

Jackson, Donald D.   Judges.   New York: Atheneum,
1974.   433p.   73-91633   KF8775. J3
Provides a critical view of a judge's role in the American legal system.

Schubert, Glendon A.   Judicial Policy Making; The Politi-
cal Role of the Courts.   Rev. ed.   Glenview, Ill. :
Scott, Foresman, 1974.   239p.   73-82373 KF8700. Z9S34
1974
Details the relationship of law and politics in the
United States.

JUSTICE, ADMINISTRATION OF

Lieberman, Jethro K.   How the Government Breaks the
Law.   New York: Stein and Day, 1972.   309p.
75-186818   KF384. L5
A critical examination of justice and politics in the
United States.   Discusses the administrative aspects of
criminal justice.

Lobenthal, Joseph S.   Power and Put-on; The Law in
America.   New York: Outerbridge & Dienstfrey, 1971
(dist. by Dutton).   187p.   72-126583   KF8700. Z9L6
Discusses the political role of judicial administration
in the United States.

Logan, Albert B.   Justice in Jeopardy; Strategy to Revita-
lize the American Dream.   Springfield, Ill.:   Thomas,
1973.   243p.   72-88485   KF8700. L6
Outlines a method of placing the American judicial system on its designed track.

LATIN AMERICA--POLITICS

Beyond Cuba: Latin America Takes Charge of Its Future.
Edited by Luigi R. Einaudi.   New York: Crane, Rus-
sak, 1974.   250p.   73-86440   F1414. 2. B45   1974
Most of the papers were originally presented at a conference on "Trends in Latin America," organized by
the Rand Corp. and held at Airlie House, Warrenton,
Va. , May 12-14, 1972.

Denton, Charles F.   Latin American Politics: A Functional Approach.   With Breston L. Lawrence.   San
Francisco: Chandler Pub. Co. , 1972.   242p.
74-179035   JL960. D47
Describes Latin American politics since 1948 within a
functional perspective.

Martz, John D. , ed.   The Dynamics of Change in Latin
American Politics.   2d ed.   Englewood Cliffs, N. J. :
Prentice-Hall, 1971.   395p.   74-138482   F1414. 2. M27
1971
A group of papers describing the Latin American politi-
cal process emphasizing social conditions.

Ranis, Peter.   Five Latin American Nations; A Comparative Political Study.   New York: Macmillan, 1971.
337p.   70-123453   F1410. R334
A comparative survey of problems within five leading
Latin American countries.

Solaún, Mauricio.   Sinners and Heretics; The Politics of
Military Intervention in Latin America.   With Michael
A. Quinn.   Urbana: University of Illinois Press, 1973.
228p.   72-78402   F1414. 2. S64
This study focuses on the role of the military in South
American politics.

Von Lazar, Arpad J.   Latin American Politics: A Primer.   Boston: Allyn and Bacon, 1971.   157p.   79-116431
JL953 1971. V63

An introductory exploration of Latin American politics since 1948.

LAW

Colby, Edward E.   Everything You've Always Wanted to Know About the Law but Couldn't Afford to Ask.   New York: Drake Publishers, 1972.   267p.   72-2780 KF387. C54
A popular treatment of everyday legal problems in the United States.

Diamond, Arthur S.   The Evolution of Law and Order. Westport, Conn.: Greenwood Press, 1973.   342p. 72-9372.   No. LC classification given.
A reprint of an important work on primitive law and its historical development.   First published in 1951.

Dolan, Edward F.   Legal Action; A Layman's Guide. Chicago: Regnery, 1972.   299p.   73-183802 KF387. D58
Discusses common legal problems that affect the layman.

Fisher, Bruce D.   Introduction to the Legal System: Theory, Overview, Business Applications.   St. Paul: West Pub. Co., 1972.   621p.   72-81197   KF385.A4F58
A basic and detailed introduction to law in the United States.

Mermin, Samuel.   Law and the Legal System; An Introduction.   Boston: Little, Brown, 1973.   339p. 73-6409   KF380. M47
Clearly explains the U. S. legal system.

Post, Charles G.   An Introduction to the Law.   Englewood Cliffs, N. J.: Prentice-Hall, 1963.   185p. 63-20413   No. LC classification given.
Explains the function and role of law in the United States.

LEGISLATIVE BODIES

Grumm, John G.   A Paradigm for the Comparative Analysis of Legislative Systems.   Beverly Hills, Calif.:

Sage Publications, 1973.   83p.   73-92220   JF511.G84
Outlines a conceptual approach for the comparative analysis of legislative bodies.

Robinson, James A.   State Legislative Innovation; Case
Studies of Washington, Ohio, Florida, Illinois, Wisconsin, and California.   New York: Praeger, 1973.   281p.
73-8172   JK2484.R6
Using case studies this work emphasizes the innova-
tions in the legislative processes of state governments
in the United States.

Rosenthal, Alan.   Legislative Performance in the States;
Explorations of Committee Behavior.   New York: Free
Press, 1974.   215p.   73-10576   JK2495.R67
Develops the role of state legislatures and their com-
mittee structures.

LIBERALISM, POLITICAL ASPECTS

Cumming, Robert D.   Human Nature and History; A Study
of the Development of Liberal Political Thought.   Chicago: University of Chicago Press, 1969.   2v.
68-54081   JC571.C77
A detailed survey of liberal thought.

Pfaff, William.   Condemned to Freedom.   New York:
Random House, 1971.   210p.   70-143995   JC571.P44
Develops the role of liberal thought and the issue of
freedom.

Strauss, Leo.   Liberalism, Ancient and Modern.   New
York: Basic Books, 1968.   276p.   68-54139   JC585.S76
A classic survey of liberalism and political thought.

LIBERTY

Cranston, Maurice W.   Freedom.   3d ed.   New York:
Basic Books, 1967.   131p.   68-20961   JC585.C68
1967b
A brief study of liberty and freedom in political thought.

Hospers, John.   Libertarianism: A Political Philosophy
for Tomorrow.   Los Angeles: Nash Pub., 1971.
488p.   71-127482   JC585.H78

Analyzes the origins of liberty and the limits of laissez-faire.

Kallen, Horace M. A Study of Liberty. Westport, Conn. : Greenwood Press, 1973. 151p. 72-7964 JC585. K26 1973
A reprint of a general survey on liberty and freedom in history. First published in 1959.

Laski, Harold J. Liberty in the Modern State. Clifton, N. J. : A. M. Kelley, 1972. 175p. 77-122064 JC585. L3 1972
A classic treatment on liberty and political thought. First published in 1948.

Rothbard, Murray N. For a New Liberty. New York: Macmillan, 1973. 327p. 72-87165 JC599. U5R66
Details liberty, laissez-faire, along with social and economic policy in the United States.

LOBBYING

Deakin, James. The Lobbyists. Washington, D. C. : Public Affairs Press, 1966. 309p. 66-25663 JK1118. D4
The history of lobbying with brief character sketches of some lobbyists.

Dexter, Lewis A. How Organizations Are Represented in Washington. Indianapolis: Bobbs-Merrill, 1969. 157p. 69-15729 JK1118. D45
Reviews the patterns of lobbying in the American political system.

Farkas, Suzanne. Urban Lobbying; Mayors in the Federal Arena. New York: New York University Press, 1971. 335p. 77-124523 JK1118. F36
Explores the work of lobbyists on the local level and their attempts to influence national policy.

Murphy, Thomas P. Pressures Upon Congress; Legislation by Lobby. Woodbury, N. Y. : Barron's Educational Series, Inc. , 1973. 136p. 72-7681 JK1118. M85
Examines the pressure of lobbyists on the Congress.

Truman, David B.   The Governmental Process; Political
Interests and Public Opinion.   2d ed.   New York:
Knopf, 1971.   544p.   78-150772   JK1118. T7   1971
Discusses politics or group conflict.   A widely used
analysis.

Wilson, James Q.   Political Organizations.   New York:
Basic Books, 1974.   359p.   73-85991   JK1118. W54
Details the role of lobbyists and various pressure
groups in American politics.

LOCAL GOVERNMENT

Alderfer, Harold F.   Local Government in Developing
Countries.   New York: McGraw-Hill, 1964.   251p.
63-20718   JS78. A4
A comparative study of local governments in underdeveloped areas.

Downes, Bryan T. , comp.   Cities and Suburbs: Selected
Readings in Local Politics and Public Policy.   Belmont, Calif. :   Wadsworth Pub. Co. , 1971.   500p.
71-140752   JS323. D66
A collection of essays on U. S. local and municipal
government.

Torrence, Susan W.   Grass Roots Government; The
County in American Politics.   Washington: R. B.
Luce, 1974.   243p.   72-97709   JS411. T67
Outlines the role of county government in American
politics.

LOCKE, JOHN

Two Treatises on Government.   A classic of political
philosophy.   There are a number of editions available.

MACHIAVELLI, NICCOLO

The Prince.   A classic work in the field of political
thought.   There are many editions available.

MIDDLE EAST--POLITICS

Allen, Sir Richard H. S. Imperialism and Nationalism in
    the Fertile Crescent; Sources and Prospects of the
    Arab-Israeli Conflict. New York: Oxford University
    Press, 1974. 686p. 73-90373 DS119.7.A6437
    Discusses the foundation of Jewish-Arab conflicts.

Evron, Yair. The Middle East: Nations, Superpowers,
    and Wars. New York: Praeger, 1973. 248p. 73-757
    LS119.7.E97
    A critical review of Jewish-Arab relations and Middle
    East politics.

Hurewitz, Jacob C. Middle East Politics: The Military
    Dimension. New York: Octagon Books, 1974. 550p.
    73-22034 DS62.8.H8 1974
    Presents the role of the military in Middle East poli-
    tics. First published in 1969.

Ismael, Tareq Y. The Middle East in World Politics; A
    Study in Contemporary International Relations. Syra-
    cuse, N.Y.: Syracuse University Press, 1974. 297p.
    73-16637 DS62.8.I84
    This collection of essays discusses the problems of
    Middle East foreign relations.

al-Marayati, Abid A. The Middle East: Its Governments
    and Politics. Belmont, Calif.: Duxbury Press, 1972.
    491p. 72-75342 DS63.1.M34
    A somewhat comparative analysis of various Middle
    Eastern governments.

Political Dynamics in the Middle East. Edited by Paul Y.
    Hammond and Sidney S. Alexander. New York:
    American Elsevier Pub. Co., 1972. 666p. 71-161688
    DS63.1.P65
    A collection of critical readings dealing both with eco-
    nomic and political problems and prospects.

Rustow, Dankwart A. Middle Eastern Political Systems.
    Englewood Cliffs, N.J.: Prentice-Hall, 1971. 114p.
    75-126829 JF51.R84
    A brief comparative analysis of the governments of the
    Middle East.

MILL, JOHN STUART

On Liberty. A classic work in political philosophy.
There are many editions available.

MINORITIES, POLITICAL ACTIVITY

Garcia, F. Chris, comp. Chicano Politics: Readings.
New York: MSS Information Corp. , 1973. 224p.
72-11569 E184. M5G36
A critical collection of essays on Chicano politics and
suffrage.

Harzog, Stephen J. , comp. Minority Group Politics; A
Reader. New York: Holt, Rinehart and Winston,
1971. 358p. 78-138408 E184. A1H48
A group of readings covering the broad scope of race
relations and politics in the United States.

Holden, Matthew. The Politics of the Black "Nation. "
New York: Chandler Pub. Co. , 1973. 75-166571
E185. 615. H58
Details black political perspectives.

Minorities in Politics. Greenville, N. C. : Department of
Political Science, East Carolina University, 1973.
101p. 73-75677 JF1061. M55
A brief collection of readings emphasizing political
participation.

Walton, Hanes. Black Politics; A Theoretical and Structural Analysis. Philadelphia: Lippincott, 1972.
246p. 72-155878 E185. 61. W193
A conceptual analysis by a black scholar.

MONTESQUIEU, CHARLES LOUIS DE SECONDAT

Spirit of the Laws. A classic of political thought. Many
editions are available.

MUNICIPAL GOVERNMENT

Adrian, Charles R. Governing Urban America. With
Charles Press. 4th ed. New York: McGraw-Hill,

1972. 577p. 70-37086 JS331.A4 1972
An in-depth survey of municipal government in the
United States.

Cole, Richard L. Citizen Participation and the Urban
Policy Process. Lexington, Mass.: Lexington Books,
1974. 178p. 73-18246 JS341.C64 1974
Focuses on the problems of municipal government and
decentralization.

Dye, Thomas R., ed. Politics in the Metropolis; A
Reader in Conflict and Cooperation. Edited with Brett
W. Hawkins. 2d ed. Columbus, Ohio: Merrill, 1971.
542p. 79-139964 JS341.D8 1971
This collection of interpretive essays focuses on social
problems and municipal government.

Goodnow, Frank J. City Government in the United States.
New York: Arno Press, 1974. 315p. 73-11903
JS331.G7 1974
A basic analysis of municipal government in the United
States. A reprint of the 1904 edition.

Gordon, Daniel N., comp. Social Change and Urban Politics; Readings. Englewood Cliffs, N.J.: Prentice-Hall,
1973. 318p. 72-1847 JS341.G67
This collection of essays deals with social conditions
as related to local and municipal government.

Hawley, Willis D. Improving the Quality of Urban Management. Edited with David Rogers. Beverly Hills,
Calif.: Sage Publications, 1974. 639p.
Readings which cover the broad scope of municipal
government and services.

Lewis, Eugene. The Urban Political System. Hinsdale,
Ill.: Dryden Press, 1973. 328p. 72-14008 JS341.L43
Focuses on community power and municipal affairs.

Lineberry, Robert L. Urban Politics and Public Policy.
With Ira Sharkansky. 2d ed. New York: Harper &
Row, 1974. 348p. 73-15418 JS422.L54 1974
Clearly explains the role of public policy in urban poli-
tics.

National Municipal League. Committee on Metropolitan
Government. The Government of Metropolitan Areas

in the United States.   Prepared by Paul Studenski.
New York: Arno Press, 1974.   403p.   73-11922
JS422.N38   1974
Discusses the basic problems of metropolitan areas in
the United States.   A reprint of the 1930 ed.

Organizing Public Services in Metropolitan America.   Edited by Thomas P. Murphy and Charles R. Warren.
Lexington, Mass. :   Lexington Books, 1974.   245p.
74-307   JS422.O73
These essays trace the development of municipal services in the United States.

Russell, John R.   Cases in Urban Management.   Cambridge, Mass. :   MIT Press, 1974.   556p.   73-20228
JS356.R95
Using the case study approach discusses the management of municipal services.

Stedman, Murray S.   Urban Politics.   Cambridge, Mass. :
Winthrop Publishers, 1972.   329p.   70-181334
JS323.S84
Scholarly and up-to-date survey of urban political
problems.

Upson, Lent D.   Practice of Municipal Administration.
New York: Arno Press, 1974.   588p.   73-11912
JS78.U6   1974
Deals with the administrative aspects of municipal
government.   A reprint of the 1926 edition.

Wilcox, Delos F.   Great Cities in America: Their Problems and Their Government.   New York: Arno Press,
1974.   426p.   73-11907   JS331.W54   1974
Focuses on the basic problems of municipal governments.   A reprint of the 1910 ed.

Zimmerman, Joseph F.   The Federated City; Community
Control in Large Cities.   New York: St. Martin's
Press, 1973.   114p.   72-91275   JS341.Z54

Zueblin, Charles.   American Municipal Progress.   New
York: Arno Press, 1974.   522p.   73-11931
JS341.Z8   1974
A basic survey of municipal government.   A reprint
of the 1916 ed.

NATIONALISM

Deutsch, Karl W.   Nationalism and Its Alternatives.   New
York: Knopf, 1969.   200p.   69-15838   JC311.D42
Clearly presents and explains the development of na-
tionalism in the contemporary world.

Hinsley, Francis H.   Nationalism and the International
System.   Dobbs Ferry, N.Y.: Oceana Publications,
1973.   192p.   72-13539   JC311.H57   1973
Relates the background of nationalistic and international-
istic movements.

Shafer, Boyd C.   Faces of Nationalism; New Realities and
Old Myths.   New York: Harcourt Brace Jovanovich,
1972.   535p.   72-174514   JC311.S477
A broad historical survey.

Smith, Anthony Douglas.   Theories of Nationalism.   New
York: Harper & Row, 1971.   344p.   73-181528
JC311.S54   1971b
Discusses the conceptual processes involved in nation-
alism.

Snyder, Louis L.   The Meaning of Nationalism.   New
York: Greenwood Press, 1968.   208p.   68-8338
JC311.S55   1968
A reprint of an important general survey.   First pub-
lished in 1954.

OBLIGATION, POLITICAL

Flathman, Richard E.   Political Obligation.   New York:
Atheneum, 1972.   334p.   75-181460   JC328.F54
A basic survey of political obligation with emphasis on
its theoretical aspects.

Hanson, Donald W., comp.   Obligation and Dissent: An
Introduction to Politics.   With Robert B. Fowler.
Boston: Little, Brown, 1971.   389p.   70-151010
JC328.H3
A group of readings focusing on the problem of dissent
and obligation in the political arena.

Political and Legal Obligation.   Edited by J. Roland Pennock and John W. Chapman.   New York: Atherton

Press, 1970.   455p.   70-105609   JC328.P58
These essays develop the problem of allegiance and
resistance to governmental authority.

OPPOSITION, POLITICAL

McLennan, Barbara N.   Political Opposition and Dissent.
New York: Dunellen Pub. Co., 1973.   393p.   72-91993
JC328.3.M36
Considers the role of dissent in political regimes and
how it is handled by different types of governments.

PLATO

The Republic.   One of the classics of political philosophy.
There are many editions available.

POLITICAL PARTICIPATION

Coplin, William D.   Everyman's Prince; A Guide to Un-
derstanding Your Political Problems.   With Michael
K. O'Leary and John Vasquez.   North Scituate, Mass.:
Duxbury Press, 1972.   185p.   72-75111   JK2274.A3C65
A basic guide for those who would better understand
practical politics in the U.S.

Golembiewski, Robert T., comp.   Dilemmas of Political
Participation; Issues for Thought and Simulations for
Action.   Edited with J. M. Moore and Jack Rabin.
Englewood Cliffs, N.J.:   Prentice-Hall, 1973.   355p.
72-10248   JK2274.A3G64
A collection of relevant essays on citizen participation
with emphasis upon simulation methods.

Gurr, Ted R.   Political Performance: A Twelve-nation
Study.   With Muriel McClelland.   Beverly Hills, Calif.:
Sage Publications, 1971.   87p.   72-167877   JA74.G87
A brief comparative study of political participation.

Rosenau, James N.   Citizenship Between Elections; An
Inquiry into the Mobilizable American.   New York:
Free Press, 1974.   526p.   73-16907   JK1118.R67
1974
Relates the significant aspects of political participation
to psychological forces.

Strategies for Political Participation. By Frank Kendrick
and others. 2d ed. Cambridge, Mass.: Winthrop
Publishers, 1974. 197p. 74-8085 JK2274.A3S7 1974
Outlines ways to get better citizen participation in the
American political system.

Verba, Sidney. Participation in America: Political De-
mocracy and Social Equality. With Norman H. Nie.
New York: Harper & Row, 1972. 428p. 72-80128
JK2274.A3V4
A somewhat theoretically oriented study of American
political participation.

POLITICAL PARTIES

Chase, James S. Emergence of the Presidential Nominat-
ing Convention, 1789-1832. Urbana: University of
Illinois Press, 1973. 332p. 72-97157 JK2255.C45
Examines the foundation of the American political convention system.

Cook, Fred J. The Rise of American Political Parties.
New York: F. Watts, 1971. 90p. 77-161834
JK2288.C6
Discusses the origins and growth of America's political
parties, the first of which grew out of the differences
between Alexander Hamilton and Thomas Jefferson in
1792.

Duverger, Maurice. Party Politics and Pressure Groups;
A Comparative Introduction. Translated by David
Wagoner. New York: Crowell, 1972. 168p.
77-179766 JF2011.D8813
A classical comparative study of political parties in
various nations.

James, Judson L. American Political Parties in Transi-
tion. New York: Harper & Row, 1974. 273p.
73-13301 JK2265.J34
A critical analysis of the modern party system in the
United States.

Johnson, Samuel A. Essentials of Political Parties; Their
Relation to American Government. Woodbury, N.Y.:
Barron's Educational Series, 1974. 202p. 73-8066
JK2261.J67

Outlines the development and role of political parties
and U.S. politics.

McDonald, Neil A.   The Study of Political Parties.   New
York: Random House, 1963, c1955.   97p.
NUC65-33399 No LC classification given.
A basic introduction to the functions, roles and prob-
lems of political parties.

Madron, Thomas W.   Political Parties in the United
States.   With Carl P. Chelf.   Boston: Holbrook Press,
1974.   352p.   73-87649   JK2261.M32
Investigates the growth and development of the party
system in America.

Schlesinger, Arthur M.   History of U.S. Political Parties.
New York: Chelsea House Publishers, 1973.   4v.
72-8682   JK2261.S35
An extensive and excellent historical treatise.

Sundquist, James L.   Dynamics of the Party System;
Alignment and Realignment of Political Parties in the
United States.   Washington: The Brookings Institution,
1973.   388p.   73-1083   JK2261.S9
A general and scholarly study of the American party
system and its historical development.

POLITICAL PSYCHOLOGY

Ashford, Douglas E.   Ideology and Participation.   Beverly
Hills, Calif.: Sage Publications, 1972.   300p.
72-98028   JA74.5.A8
Develops a framework for understanding the role of
ideology in political participation.

Di Renzo, Gordon J.   Personality and Politics.   Garden
City, N.Y.: Anchor Books, 1974.   539p.   73-15479
JA74.5.D55
The psychological foundations of politics and human
personality are discussed in detail.

Easton, David.   A Systems Analysis of Political Life.
New York: Wiley, 1965.   507p.   65-12714   JA74.E23
An extensive study seeking a general theory of politics.

Eulau, Heinz. The Behavioral Persuasion in Politics.
    New York: Random House, 1963. 141p. 62-21335
    JA74. E88
    A general statement of the behavioral approach to under-
    standing political behavior.

Handbook of Political Psychology. Jeanne N. Knutson,
    general editor. San Francisco: Josey-Bass Publishers,
    1973. 542p. 72-5893 JA74. 5. H35
    A collection of outstanding essays on psychological as-
    pects of political behavior.

Lane, Robert E. Political Man. New York: Free Press,
    1972. 328p. 75-158930 JA74. 5. L37
    A study of man's political nature and his behavior in
    society.

Lane, Ruth. Political Man; Toward a Conceptual Base.
    Beverly Hills, Calif.: Sage Publications, 1973. 71p.
    73-87845 JA74. 5. L38
    Introduces some of the diverse concepts and theories
    involved in political psychology.

Renshon, Stanley A. Psychological Needs and Political
    Behavior: A Theory of Personality and Political Effi-
    cacy. New York: Free Press, 1974. 300p.
    73-11735 JA74. 5. R45
    A theoretical treatise on political behavior.

Schwartz, David C. Political Alienation and Political Be-
    havior. Chicago: Aldine Pub. Co., 1973. 286p.
    70-169518 JA74. 5. S36
    Includes case studies emphasizing alienation in U. S.
    politics and government.

Stone, William F. The Psychology of Politics. New
    York: Free Press, 1974. 291p. 73-17647 JA74. 5. S8
    A general survey of political psychology and participa-
    tion in the political process.

POLITICAL SCIENCE

Allman, Joe. Creative Politics. Pacific Palisades,
    Calif.: Goodyear Pub. Co., 1972. 242p. 71-179010
    This study concentrates on problems, alternative solu-
    tions, and normative criteria for judgment in the an-
    alysis of politics.

Andrian, Charles F.   Political Life and Social Change:
An Introduction to Political Science.   2d ed.   Belmont,
Calif. : Duxbury Press, 1974.   354p.   74-75712
JA66. A53   1974
Concentrates on comparative political institutions and
social change.

Carter, Gwendolen M.   Government and Politics in the
Twentieth Century.   With John H. Herz.   3d ed.   New
York: Praeger Publishers, 1973.   278p.   72-83003
JA66. C3   1973
A well written and concise study of modern govern-
ments.   A functional treatment.

Crick, Bernard R.   Political Theory and Practice.   New
York: Basic Books, 1974.   243p.   72-89853
JA71. C72   1974
Contains a collection of his research articles covering
important recent theoretical and practical topics in po-
litical science.

Dahl, Robert A.   Modern Political Analysis.   2d ed.
Englewood Cliffs, N. J. : Prentice-Hall, 1970.   118p.
70-93290   JC330. D34   1970
A brief introduction to a rigorous, empirical study of
politics.   It is both systematic and analytical in its
approach and is intended for the introductory student.

Deutsch, Karl W.   Politics and Government; How People
Decide Their Fate.   2d ed.   Boston: Houghton Mifflin,
1974.   607p.   73-14499   JA71. D45   1974
A basic text and survey of political science and comparative government by a recognized authority.

Dragnich, Alex N. , ed.   Government and Politics; An
Introduction to Political Science.   Written with others.
2d ed.   New York: Random House, 1971.   736p.
77-124479   JA71. D7   1971
An introductory survey covering both analytical and
comparative approaches to the study of political science.
Each section is authored by a specialist.

Easton, David.   The Political System; An Inquiry into the
State of Political Science.   2d ed.   New York: Knopf,
1971.   377p.   78-137991   JA71. E3   1971
A call for an expansion and rejuvenation of the theoretical concerns of political science.   It discusses and
develops a basic orienting concept of the political.

Feld, Werner J. , comp. The Enduring Questions of Politics.   Edited with others.   2d ed.   Englewood Cliffs,
N.J.: Prentice-Hall, 1974.   336p.   73-13549 JA66.F4
1974
A collection of essays each on a specific issue in political science.

Frohock, Fred M.   Normative Political Theory.   Englewood Cliffs, N.J.: Prentice-Hall, 1974.   118p.
73-10027 JA79.F73
Develops a framework for political analysis.

Gellner, Ernest.   Contemporary Thought and Politics.
Edited with others.   Boston: Routledge & K. Paul,
1974.   207p.   73-86571 JA71.G37 1974
Considers the contemporary issues of political science
and political sociology.

Guild, Nelson Prescott, comp.   Introduction to Politics;
Essays and Readings.   Compiled with Kenneth T.
Palmer.   New York: Wiley, 1968.   341p.   67-29016
JA66.G8
The material in this book is organized around five
basic questions that are important in understanding the
nature of politics.

Hacker, Andrew.   The Study of Politics: The Western
Tradition and American Origins.   2d ed.   New York:
McGraw-Hill, 1973.   120p.   72-4851 JA81.H233   1973
This brief introduction to politics presents the Western
political tradition and focuses on the American System
to demonstrate how political theory, political institutions, and political behavior relate to each other and
to American politics.

Hitchner, Dell G.   Modern Government.   With William H.
Harbold. 3d ed. New York: Dodd, Mead, 1972.
522p.   73-180930 JA66.H5   1972
The authors attempt to introduce the reader to the
broad and complex subject of contemporary government
and politics, and to provide not only information about
the governmental process but standards for its evaluation as well.

Irish, Marian D. , comp.   Political Science; Advance of
the Discipline.   Englewood Cliffs, N.J.: Prentice-Hall,
1968.   248p.   68-7880 JA38.I74

The state of the discipline and its changes during the
past 30 years are surveyed by a number of prominent
scholars.

Jacobsen, Gertrude A.   Political Science.   With M. H.
Lipman.   New York: Barnes & Noble, 1965.   244p.
65-26063   JA66.J3   1965
A general study guide, syllabus or review manual for
students.   Frequent charts and diagrams are used to
interpret the text and a series of examination questions
and references are provided

Johnson, Samuel A.   Essentials of Political Science.   Rev.
Woodbury, N.Y. : Barron's Educational Series, Inc. ,
1971.   321p.   70-29225   JA86.J6   1971
Details in understandable language the diverse aspects
of politics.

Kariel, Henry S.   Open Systems; Arenas for Political Action.   Itasca, Ill. : F. E. Peacock Publishers, 1969.
148p.   68-57971   JA71.K32
An analysis of the problems of closure in contemporary
society and American political science.   His argument
is that "politics at its best (not all politics) is a kind
of play, of agnosistic exertion, of free and self-delight-
ing action. "

Neubauer, Deane E. , comp.   Readings in Modern Political
Analysis.   2d ed.   Englewood Cliffs, N.J. : Prentice-
Hall, 1974.   356p.   73-9736   JA71.N47   1974
A collection of essays on problems involved in political
analysis.

Palmer, Monte.   The Interdisciplinary Study of Politics.
With Larry Stern and Charles Gaile.   New York:
Harper & Row, 1974.   177p.   74-7097   JA71.P333
Analyzes the relationship of psychology, sociology and
economics to politics.   Attempts to define behavioral
concepts.

Pennock, James R.   Political Science; An Introduction.
With David G. Smith.   New York: Macmillan, 1964.
707p.   64-12866   JA71.P4
An advanced survey covering most phases of the subject, but does not include structural forms of government.

Roseman, Cyril, ed. Dimensions of Political Analysis:
An Introduction to the Contemporary Study of Politics.
Edited with others.   Englewood Cliffs, N.J.: Prentice-
Hall, 1966.   368p.   66-13643   JA71. R63
Selected readings and analysis that attempt to provide
a coherent overview of the discipline of political science.

Rosenau, James N.   The Dramas of Politics: An Introduction to the Joys of Inquiry.   Boston: Little, Brown,
1973.   250p.   72-5936   JA71. R64
This work seeks to involve students by outlining why
the study of politics is satisfying.   It does so by drawing parallels between the dramatic dimensions of politics and those of personal life, with the dynamics of
political systems being analogized to those of families,
friendships, marriages, jobs, and college campuses.

Rosenbaum, Herbert D.   A First Book in Politics and
Government.   Hinsdale, Ill.: Dryden Press, 1972.
235p.   72-187770   JA74. R63
A basic introduction written for young students.

Schmandt, Henry J.   Fundamentals of Government.   With
Paul G. Steinbicker.   2d ed.   Milwaukee: Bruce Pub.
Co., 1963.   444p.   63-17496   JA66. S35   1963
Approaches the study of political science with the con-
viction that political philosophy as well as empirically
oriented political science should be examined.

Sidjanski, Dusan.   Political Decision-Making Processes;
Studies in National, Comparative and International Poli-
tics.   New York: Elsevier Scientific Pub. Co., 1973.
237p.   74-165111   JA74. S47   1973b
Reports presented to a group of specialists at the 8th
World Congress of the International Political Science
Association, Munich, Sept. 1970.

Stevenson, Thomas H.   Politics and Government.   Totowa,
N.J.: Littlefield, Adams, 1973.   435p.   72-85271
JA66. S83
An introductory text which can be used as the nucleus
of the course in conjunction with outside reading as-
signments.

Strickland, Donald A.   A Primer of Political Analysis.
2d ed.   With L. L. Wade and R. E. Johnston.   Chicago: Markham Pub. Co., 1972.   112p.   79-174990

JA74. S7 1972
This primer is a guide to the ways of thinking about political things. It deals with fundamental notions of structure and function in politics.

Wasby, Stephen L. Political Science: The Discipline and Its Dimensions; An Introduction. With chapters by William C. Baum and others. New York: Scribner, 1970. 586p. 79-100129 JA71. W3
A useful general introduction to the field.

Welsh, William A. Studying Politics. New York: Praeger, 1973. 260p. 77-189929 JA71. W44
A concise introduction to the varied frameworks in which political life may be analyzed and understood and to the basic elements of scientific methodology used by political scientists today.

POLITICAL SCIENCE--MATHEMATICAL MODELS

Alker, Hayward R. Mathematical Approaches to Politics. Edited with Karl W. Deutsch, and Antoine H. Stoetzel. New York: Elsevier Scientific Pub. Co. , 1973. 479p. 74-171383 JA73. A39 1973b
This collection of scholarly essays details the usefulness of mathematical models in the study of politics.

_____. Mathematics and Politics. New York: Macmillan, 1965. 152p. 65-15593 JA73. A4
An introductory study of mathematical applications in political science.

Buchanan, William. Understanding Political Variables. 2d ed. New York: Scribner, 1974. 305p. 73-1347 JA73. B78 1974
A handbook and workbook on mathematical applications to political research.

Coplin, William D. Simulation in the Study of Politics. Chicago: Markham Pub. Co. , 1968. 365p. 68-15876 JA73. C65
An attempt to explain the application of simulation and its data in political research.

Kirkpatrick, Samuel A. , comp. Quantitative Analysis of Political Data. Columbus, Ohio: Merrill, 1974.

509p.   73-82657   JA73.K56
A collection of scholarly essays on mathematical
models in political science.

POLITICAL SCIENCE--METHODOLOGY

Benson, Oliver E.   Political Science Laboratory.   Columbus, Ohio: C. E. Merrill Pub. Co. , 1969.   402p.
69-10596   JA73.B38
An introductory manual covering the basic elements of
a quantitative political science paper, which requires
no mathematics background beyond use of tables and
graphs, yet is still advanced enough to be well worth-
while.

Contemporary Political Science: Toward Empirical Theory.
Edited by Ithiel de Sola Pool.   New York: McGraw-
Hill, 1967.   276p.   67-21592   JA73.C63
A group of nine essays which attempt to illuminate the
essential intellectual anarchy of the discipline and illustrate how the increasing pervasiveness of the scientific
approach is both a symptom and a cause of that anarchy.

Everson, David H.   An Introduction to Systematic Political Science.   Homewood, Ill.: Dorsey Press, 1973.
296p.   72-93549   JA73.E84
A basic introduction to the key concepts of political
science.

Falco, Maria J.   Truth and Meaning in Political Science;
An Introduction to Political Inquiry.   Columbus, Ohio:
Merrill, 1973.   150p.   73-75328   JA73.F34
Introduces the student to basic methodology both in po-
litical science and social science in general.

Frohock, Fred M.   The Nature of Political Inquiry.
Homewood, Ill.: Dorsey Press, 1967.   218p.   67-
21010   H61.F67
Among the topics included in this study are the episte-
mological premises of logical positivism and meta-
physics; the nature of functional and causal explana-
tions; the characteristics of scientific social analysis;
the role of values in political behavior and analysis.

Isaak, Alan C.   Scope and Methods of Political Science;
An Introduction to the Methodology of Political Inquiry.

Homewood, Ill. : Dorsey Press, 1969. 257p.
70-90240 JA71.I75
The main objective of this study is to provide a methodological foundation for reading, understanding, and crit-
icizing the literature of political science and in doing
political research.

Lasswell, Harold D. Power and Society; A Framework
for Political Inquiry. With Abraham Kaplan. New
Haven: Yale University Press, 1950. 295p. 50-10115
JC251.L27
A valuable essay supplying political science with a body
of precise definitions and significant scientific proposi-
tions.

Leege, David C. Political Research: Design, Measurement, and Analysis. With Wayne L. Francis. New
York: Basic Books, 1974. 417p. 73-82232 JA73.L43
A comprehensive text and reference guide to the basic
tools of contemporary political research.

Meehan, Eugene J. The Foundations of Political Analysis:
Empirical and Normative. Homewood, Ill. : Dorsey
Press, 1971. 274p. 70-149910 JA71.M365
Offering a behavioral approach to the problem of studying political thought, this critical, analytic study provides a conceptual structure or analytic framework in
relation to the thought of a particular time period. In
effect it studies current discussions of methodological,
conceptual and evaluative problems in the study of politics.

Payne, James L. Foundations of Empirical Political Analysis. Chicago: Markham Pub. Co. , 1973. 150p.
72-95720 JA73.P38
The aim of this study is to treat the common episte-
mological problems social scientists actually face in
their writing and research.

Van Dyke, Vernon. Political Science: A Philosophical
Analysis. Stanford, Calif. : Stanford University Press,
1960. 235p. 60-11836 JA73.V3
The author presents and supports his belief that the
study of politics should be pursued with the objectives
of natural science and discusses the methods appropriate to this enterprise.

Young, Roland A. , ed. Approaches to the Study of Politics. Evanston, Ill. : Northwestern University Press, 1958. 382p. 58-5518 JA37.46
A collection of 22 essays by leading political scientists, dealing with the nature of politics and the methodology of its study.

POLITICAL SCIENCE--STUDY AND TEACHING

Behavioral and Social Sciences Survey Committee. Political Science Panel. Political Science. Edited by Heinz Eulau and James G. March. Englewood Cliffs, N. J. : Prentice-Hall, 1969. 148p. 79-96971 JA88.U6B45
This volume describes the significant past achievements of political science, and indicates its vast potential for the future. Both theoretical and applied political science are considered.

Crick, Bernard. The American Science of Politics: Its Origins and Conditions. Berkeley: University of California Press, 1959. 252p. 59-3487rev. JA84.U5C7
A useful and critical evaluation of American political science and its tendencies.

Hyneman, Charles S. The Study of Politics: The State of American Political Science. Urbana: University of Illinois Press, 1959. 232p. 59-10554 JA84.U5H9
A balanced, no-nonsense description of American political science. Specific attention is given to what political scientists study and the intellectual conflicts within the field.

Merritt, Richard L. The Student Political Scientist's Handbook. With Gloria J. Pyszka. Cambridge, Mass. : Schenkman Pub. Co. , 1969. 171p. 70-79681 JA86.M4
Briefly discusses politics as a subject of investigation including the various areas of study within the field and career opportunities. The authors attempt to assist students in their preparation of term papers, guides them to bibliographies, reference books and periodical literature. They also describe how to formulate a research thesis, perform research and how to organize the results of research.

Murphy, Robert E. The Style and Study of Political Science. Glenview, Ill. : Scott, Foresman, 1970. 135p.

72-94880   JA88. U6M84
What this book does attempt is to relate political science to the intellectual environment of students in order to show them what is involved in survey course work.

Schattschneider, Elmer E.   A Guide to the Study of Public Affairs.   With Victor Jones and Stephen K. Bailey. Westport, Conn. : Greenwood Press, 1973.   135p. 73-1406   JA86. S35   1973
A useful introduction, particularly for the beginning student.   A reprint of the 1952 ed.

Somit, Albert.   The Development of American Political Science: From Burgess to Behavioralism.   With Joseph Tanenhaus.   Boston: Allyn and Bacon, 1967. 220p.   67-17759   JA84. U5S63
An excellent discussion of the development of American political science and its trends.

Strum, Philippa.   On Studying Political Science.   With Michael Shmidman.   Pacific Palisades, Calif. : Goodyear Pub. Co. , 1969.   90p.   69-17982   JA86. S8
Provides an introduction to political science as a discipline, acquainting students with the areas covered in the field, its relationship to the other social sciences, the kinds of studies undertaken by political scientists, and basic methodologies, concepts and research tools.

Weissberg, Robert.   Political Learning, Political Choice, and Democratic Citizenship.   Englewood Cliffs, N. J. : Prentice-Hall, 1974.   205p.   74-630   JA88. U6W44
Discusses the training of citizens and the development of political expertise.

POLITICAL SCIENCE--TERMINOLOGY

Cranston, Maurice W. , ed.   A Glossary of Political Ideas.   With Sanford A. Lakoff.   New York: Basic Books, 1969.   180p.   76-78455   JA61. C7   1969
A basic glossary of 51 terms related to political studies.   Includes bibliographies with each entry.

Gregor, A. James.   An Introduction to Metapolitics; A Brief Inquiry into the Conceptual Language of Political Science.   New York: Free Press, 1971.   403p. 71-142363   JA61. G7

An introduction to a range of problems central to political inquiry related to language and terminology.

Weldon, Thomas D.   The Vocabulary of Politics.   Baltimore, Md. :   Penguin Books, 1953.   199p.   A55-3000
JA66. W45V
A classic treatment of the problems involved in political language.

POLITICAL SCIENCE RESEARCH

American Political Science Association.   Research Committee.   Research in Political Science.   Edited by Ernest S. Griffith.   Port Washington, N. Y. :   Kennikat
Press, 1969.   238p.   77-86021   JA86. A5   1969
A group of essays which reflectively discuss significant
aspects and observed trends in the field.   A reprint of
the 1948 ed.

Introduction to Problem Solving in Political Science.   By
Sotirios A. Barber and others.   Columbus, Ohio:
Merrill, 1971.   109p.   74-150128   JA86. I5
Discusses opinion analysis, research techniques and library resources.   The book is designed for use as a
process-of-inquiry supplement to any survey introduction to political science.

Janda, Kenneth.   Data Processing; Applications to Political Research.   2d ed.   Evanston, Ill. :   Northwestern
University Press, 1969.   294p.   76-12332   JA73. J3
1969
This handbook is designed as an introduction to the use
of modern data processing in political research.   Particular attention is paid to ways in which information
can be recorded, organized, and manipulated.

Jones, Endsley T.   Conducting Political Research.   New
York: Harper & Row, 1971.   221p.   75-165026
JA86. J63
A work on methodology for the student with no statistical background.   The author discusses the primary
topics of political research.   It is organized according
to a typical research project along with a case study
in political research which demonstrates how the elements of the research project interrelate.

McClosky, Herbert.   Political Inquiry; The Nature and
Uses of Survey Research.   New York: Macmillan,
1969.   163p.   69-18817   JA73. M32
Presents three articles which are clear statements on
the topics of survey research.

Madron, Thomas W.   Small Group Methods and the Study
of Politics.   Evanston, Ill. :   Northwestern University
Press, 1969.   218p.   69-19597   HM133. M27
This work provides students of political science with a
working guide to the research methodology of small
group analysis.   The author details both sociometric
techniques and observational procedures relevant to the
collection of data on small groups within the political
system.

Meehan, Eugene J.   The Theory and Method of Political
Analysis.   Homewood, Ill. :   Dorsey Press, 1965.
277p.   65-22418   JA71. M37
An introduction to the uses of scientific explanation in
political science.

Research Frontiers in Politics and Government.   By
Stephen K. Bailey and others.   Westport, Conn. :
Greenwood Press, 1973.   240p.   72-7820   JA86. R4
1973
A group of essays exploring the tendencies in political
science currently, its research techniques and their
limitations.   A reprint of the 1965 ed.

Shively, W. Phillips.   The Craft of Political Research:
A Primer.   Englewood Cliffs, N. J. :   Prentice-Hall
1974.   174p.   73-13500   JA73. S49
This work offers coverage of principles underlying research analysis in the field.

Wirt, Frederick M.   Introductory Problems in Political
Research.   With Roy D. Morey and Louis F. Brake-
man.   Englewood Cliffs, N. J. :   Prentice-Hall, 1970.
194p.   76-95889   JA71. W48
This work challenges the student's creative insights by
involving him directly in important problems of contemporary political research.

POLITICAL SOCIALIZATION

Adler, Norman, comp. The Learning of Political Be-
havior. With Charles Harrington. Glenview, Ill. :
Scott, Foresman, 1970. 208p. 70-100984 JA76.A32
A collection of interpretative essays.

Dawson, Richard E. Political Socialization: An Analytic
Study. With Kenneth Prewitt. Boston: Little, Brown,
1969. 226p. 69-12677 JA76.D33
An analysis of basic principles in the politicization of
people.

Dennis, Jack, comp. Socialization to Politics: A Reader.
New York: Wiley, 1973. 527p. 72-8329 JA76.D43
A group of important readings in the field.

Easton, David. Children in the Political System: Origins
of Political Legitimacy. With Jack Dennis. New York:
McGraw-Hill, 1969. 440p. 68-58506 JA76.E3
Traces the critical period of the socialization process.

Jaros, Dean. Socialization to Politics. New York:
Praeger, 1973. 160p. 70-189911 JA76.J36
Attempts to place socialization research within the con-
text of the more general study of political attitudes.

POLITICAL SOCIOLOGY

Almond, Gabriel A. Crisis, Choice, and Change; Histori-
cal Studies of Political Development. Edited with Scott
C. Flanagan and Robert J. Mundt. Boston: Little,
Brown, 1973. 717p. 72-8267 JA76.A46 1973
A collection of case studies focusing on social change.

Bowman, Lewis, comp. Political Behavior and Public
Opinion; Comparative Analyses. Edited with G. R.
Boynton. Englewood Cliffs, N. J. : Prentice-Hall,
1974. 499p. 73-1921 JA76.B69
A group of essays on comparative political institutions
in their social framework.

Dowse, Robert E. Political Sociology. With John A.
Hughes. New York: Wiley, 1972. 457p. 76-39229
JA76.D68

A critical and comprehensive review of developments in the field.

Horowitz, Irving L.   Foundations of Political Sociology. New York: Harper & Row, 1972.   590p.   78-187052 JA76.H67
Considers the basic principles in political behavior.

Lipset, Seymour M.   Political Man; The Social Bases of Politics.   Garden City, N.Y.: Doubleday, 1960. 432p.   60-5943   JC423.L58
A classic study of the sociological basis of politics.

Michels, Robert.   First Lectures in Political Sociology. New York: Arno Press, 1974.   173p.   73-14172 JA76.M52   1974
Reprint of the 1949 ed.   Considered a classic work in the field.

Perspectives in Political Sociology.   Edited by Andrew Effrat.   Indianapolis: Bobbs-Merrill Co., 1973. 311p.   73-4329   JA76.P44
These articles outline the different approaches to the field.

Reynolds, Henry T.   Politics and the Common Man; An Introduction to Political Behavior.   Homewood, Ill.: Dorsey Press, 1974.   288p.   74-76457   JA76.R48
This study is a basic introduction to political participation and the role of public opinion.

Segal, David R.   Society and Politics; Uniformity and Diversity in Modern Democracy.   Glenview, Ill.: Scott, Foresman, 1974.   206p.   73-91227   JA76.S39
A general survey of political sociology.

POLITICAL STATISTICS

Gurr, Ted R.   Politimetrics: An Introduction to Quantitative Macropolitics.   Englewood Cliffs, N.J.: Prentice-Hall, 1972.   214p.   72-1130   JA73.G87
Emphasizes the many approaches to political data manipulation.

Key, Vladimer O.   A Primer of Statistics for Political Scientists.   With a foreword by Frank Munger.   New York: Crowell, 1966.   209p.   66-24297   JA74.K48

1966
A classic in the field, this work devotes specific attention to election data.

Rai, Kul B.   Political Science Statistics.   With John C.
    Blydenburgh.   Boston: Holbrook Press, 1973.   255p.
    72-91545   JA74.R26
    Covers the basic statistical functions related to political
    data.

POLITICAL THOUGHT

Blackstone, William T.   Political Philosophy: An Intro-
    duction.   New York: Crowell, 1973.   266p.   72-13723
    JA66.B5
    A general survey of political philosophy.

Bluhm, William T.   Ideologies and Attitudes: Modern
    Political Culture.   Englewood Cliffs, N.J.:   Prentice-
    Hall, 1974.   385p.   73-16236   JC348.B55
    Examines the factors involved in the development of
    political ideologies.

Cranston, Maurice W., ed.   Western Political Philoso-
    phers.   Chester Springs, Pa.:   Dufour Editions, 1964.
    124p.   64-21415   JA81.C64
    Presents brief introductions to the essential ideas of
    the major figures who have shaped Western political
    thought.

Gould, James A., comp.   Political Ideologies.   Compiled
    with Willis H. Truitt.   New York: Macmillan, 1973.
    495p.   72-81653   JA83.G67
    Covers the broad history of political thought empha-
    sizing ideologies.

Harmon, Mont J.   Political Thought: From Plato to the
    Present.   New York: McGraw-Hill, 1964.   469p.
    63-20724   JA81.H3
    A sound and balanced general survey of political
    thought.

Hill, Paul T.   A Theory of Political Coalitions in Simple
    and Policymaking Situations.   Beverly Hills, Calif.:
    Sage Publications, 1973.   46p.   73-87851   JC330.H54

A brief theoretical analysis of political coalitions and
their role in policymaking.

Jenkin, Thomas P.   The Study of Political Theory.   New
York: Random House, 1961.   99p.   No LC Card number given.   JA71.J4   1961
This study is concerned with the main concepts in political thought and with major outlines it has assumed
in its historical development.

Kateb, George.   Political Theory; Its Nature and Uses.
New York: St. Martin's Press, 1968.   102p.
68-23034   JA71.K34
This study discusses some of the questions political
theorists have traditionally asked, and the sorts of
answers they have given.

Knowledge and Belief in Politics: the Problem of Ideology.
Edited by Robert Benewick, R. N. Berki and B. Parekh.
New York: St. Martin's Press, 1973.   327p.   73-85266
HM24.K588   1973
A collection of essays covering political ideologies and
their effect upon politics.

Sabine, George H.   A History of Political Theory.   4th
ed.   Rev. by Thomas L. Thorson.   Hinsdale, Ill.:
Dryden Press, 1973.   871p.   73-2795   JA81.S3   1973
This classic work has been revised and brought up to
date to include the most recent in political thought including that of Mao Tse-tung.

Taylor, Richard.   Freedom, Anarchy, and the Law; an
Introduction to Political Philosophy.   Englewood Cliffs,
N.J.: Prentice-Hall, 1973.   144p.   72-12832
JA71.T38
A non-historical introduction to political philosophy fo-
cusing on five basic philosophical problems.

Tinder, Glenn E.   Political Thinking; The Perennial
Questions.   2d ed.   Boston: Little, Brown, 1974.
206p.   73-13369   JA81.T56   1974
A basic discussion on political analysis stressing major questions.

Zoll, Donald A.   Twentieth Century Political Philosophy.
Englewood Cliffs, N.J.: Prentice-Hall, 1974.   190p.
74-3161   JA83.Z64

A survey of contemporary political thinkers and their
effect upon modern politics.

POLITICS, PRACTICAL

Hoopes, Roy.   Getting with Politics; A Guide to Political
Action for Young People.   New York: Delacorte Press,
1968.   209p.   67-19761   JK1976. H6
Outlines a plan for teenagers to become involved in
American politics.

Kariel, Henry S.   The Promise of Politics.   Englewood
Cliffs, N. J. :   Prentice-Hall, 1966.   120p.   66-22806
JA74. K3
A critical review of political behavior and practical
politics.

Muehl, William.   Politics in Action: How to Make Change
Happen.   New York: Association Press, 1972.   159p.
72-4054   JK1976. M8
Emphasizes the role of elections in the U. S. political
system.

Theis, Paul A.   All About Politics; Questions and
Answers on the U. S. Political Process.   With William
L. Steponkus.   New York: Bowker, 1972.   228p.
72-8470   JK1726. T48
A question and answer approach to political participa-
tion.

Walzer, Michael.   Political Action; A Practical Guide to
Movement Politics.   Chicago: Quadrangle Books, 1971.
125p.   79-143571   JF2049. W25
Summarizes a practical approach for citizen participation in practical politics.

POLLS   see   PUBLIC OPINION

POWER, POLITICAL

Bachrach, Peter, comp.   Political Elites in a Democracy.
New York: Atherton Press, 1971.   175p.   78-116534
JC330. B24
A collection of critical essays on the power of political
elites.

Berle, Adolf A. Power. New York: Harcourt, Brace & World, 1969. 603p. 79-7190 JC330.B418
A classic approach to political power with an emphasis upon its social consequences.

Champlin, John R., comp. Power. New York: Atherton Press, 1971. 194p. 71-116535 JC330.C525
A group of interpretative readings focusing upon the conceptual nature of political power.

Coleman, James S. Power and the Structure of Society. New York: Norton, 1974. 112p. 73-14727 HM136.C63
Covers the role of political power in bureaucracy, corporations, and in the civil rights movement.

Rabushka, Alvin. Politics in Plural Societies; A Theory of Democratic Instability. With Kenneth A. Shepale. Columbus, Ohio: Merrill, 1972. 232p. 71-187159 JC330.R3
A comparative study of political power in various nations.

PRESIDENTS

Bloom, Melvyn H. Public Relations and Presidential Campaigns: A Crisis in Democracy. New York: Crowell, 1973. 349p. 73-10057 JK524.B57 1973
Develops the role of public relations in presidential elections and its effect upon democratic principles.

Egger, Rowland A. The President of the United States. 2d ed. New York: McGraw-Hill, 1972. 198p. 74-174615 JK516.E33 1972
Considers the extent of executive power and the role of the presidency.

Hughes, Emmet J. The Living Presidency; The Resources and Dilemmas of the American Presidential Office. New York: Coward, McCann & Geoghegan, 1973. 377p. 72-87580 JK516.H83
Analyzes the office of the President and the dilemmas it has created in American politics.

James, Dorothy B. The Contemporary Presidency. 2d ed. Indianapolis: Pegasus, 1974. 336p. 73-19657

JK516. J33   1974
Traces the role of executive power in contemporary
American government.

Johnson, Richard T.   Managing the White House; An Inti-
    mate Study of the Presidency.   New York: Harper &
    Row, 1974,   270p.   73-5462   JK518. J63   1974.
    Focuses on staff relations within the executive branch of
    government.

Polsby, Nelson W. , comp.   The Modern Presidency.
    New York: Random House, 1973.   236p.   72-11695
    JK511. P67
    A collection of outstanding essays on the current sta-
    tus of the Presidency.

Schlesinger, Arthur M.   The Imperial Presidency.   Bos-
    ton: Houghton Mifflin, 1973.   505p.   73-15805
    JK511. S35
    A rather critical appraisal of presidential power with
    some dire predictions for the future.

Sickels, Robert J.   Presidential Transactions.   Englewood
    Cliffs, N. J. :   Prentice-Hall, 1974.   184p.   73-11012
    JK516. S5
    A critical study of the contemporary presidency.

Tugwell, Rexford G.   The Presidency Reappraised.
    Edited with Thomas E. Cronin.   New York: Praeger,
    1974.   312p.   73-6201   JK516. T82
    A current appraisal of executive power in the United
    States.

PRESSURE GROUPS

Adie, Robert F.   Latin America: The Politics of Immo-
    bility.   With Guy E. Poitras.   Englewood Cliffs, N. J. :
    Prentice-Hall, 1974.   278p.   73-7729   JL964. P7A35
    Focuses on the role of pressure groups in Latin Ameri-
    can politics.

Castles, Francis G.   Pressure Groups and Political Cul-
    ture: A Comparative Study.   New York: Humanities
    Press, 1967.   112p.   67-22209   JF529. C3
    Offers comparative analyses of pressure groups in a
    number of nations.

Interest Groups in Soviet Politics.   Edited by H. Gordon
  Skillina and Franklyn Griffiths.   Princeton, N.J.:
  Princeton University Press, 1971.   433p.   70-113014
  JN65151971. I5
  Discusses the development of pressure groups within a
  totalitarian framework.

Pym, Bridget.   Pressure Groups and the Permissive Society.   Newton Abbot: David & Charles, 1974.   183p.
  74-163023   JN329. P7P93
  Discusses pressure groups in British politics.

Zeigler, Luther H.   Interest Groups in American Society.
  With G. W. Peak.   2d ed.   Englewood Cliffs, N.J.:
  Prentice-Hall, 1972.   309p.   75-37142   JK1118Z4
  1972
  Contrasts the activities of pressure groups with the
  functions of representative government.

PROPAGANDA

Bartlett, Sir Frederic C.   Political Propaganda.   New
  York: Octagon Books, 1973.   158p.   73-8864
  HM263. B33   1973
  A reprint of the 1940 ed.   This work emphasizes the
  social consequences of political propaganda within so-
  ciety.

Childs, Harwood L., ed.   Propaganda and Dictatorship:
  A Collection of Papers.   New York: Arno Press,
  1972.   153p.   72-4659   HM263. C4   1972
  A collection of critical essays dealing with various
  aspects of propaganda in Europe between 1914 and
  1945.   A reprint of the 1936 ed.

Ellul, Jacques.   Propaganda: The Formation of Men's
  Attitudes.   Translated from the French by Konrad
  Kellen and Jean Lerner.   New York: Vintage Books,
  1973.   320p.   72-8053   HM263. E413   1973
  Examines factors involved in the development of propa-
  gandic techniques and their effect on society.

Lerner, Daniel, ed.   Propaganda in War and Crisis.
  New York: Arno Press, 1972.   500p.   72-4669
  JF1525. P8L4   1972
  A reprint of the 1951 ed. which focuses on the psycho-
  logical aspects of warfare.

Mitchell, Malcolm.   Propaganda, Polls, and Public Opin-
ion: Are the People Manipulated? Englewood Cliffs,
N. J. : Prentice-Hall, 1970. 122p.   72-169326
HM263. M58
Considers the role of advertizing as a technique of
propaganda and as it effects public opinion.

Propaganda in International Affairs.   Special editor of this
volume: L. J. Martin.   Philadelphia: American Academy of Political and Social Science, 1971.   234p.
74-169739   H1. A4   vol. 398
A collection of essays dealing with the international aspects of propaganda.

PUBLIC ADMINISTRATION

Administrative Training and Development; A Comparative
Study of East Africa, Zambia, Pakistan, and India.
Edited by Bernard Schaffer.   New York: Praeger,
1974.   445p.   73-21501   JF1338. A2A34
Presents basic case studies in public administration in-
struction.

Armstrong, John A.   The European Administrative Elite.
Princeton, N. J. : Princeton University Press, 1973.
406p.   72-6522   JF1411. A73
Investigates the administrative activities of elites in
Europe and their role in economic development.

Bartholomew, Paul C.   Public Administration.   3d ed.
Totowa, N. J. : Littlefield, Adams, 1972.   152p.
72-90923   JF1351. B27
An introductory outline of public administration and its
functions in the political system.

Kim, Jae T. , comp.   New Perspectives in Public Administration: Introductory Readings.   New York: MSS
Information Corp. , 1973.   229p.   73-14891   JF1321. K54
Presents essays on basic aspects of contemporary public administration.

Nigro, Felix A.   Modern Public Administration.   With
Lloyd G. Nigro.   3d ed.   New York: Harper & Row,
1973.   468p.   73-2702   JF1351. N5   1973
A basic text detailing the field in depth.

Rehfuss, John. Public Administration as Political Process. New York: Scribner, 1973. 247p. 72-11106 JF1351.R46
A critical analysis of public administration and U.S. politics and government.

Self, Peter. Administrative Theories and Politics; An Inquiry into the Structure and Processes of Modern Government. Toronto: University of Toronto Press, 1973. 308p. 72-98025 JF1351.S44 1973
Develops a framework for the study of public administration.

PUBLIC LAW

Abraham, Henry J. The Judicial Process; An Introductory Analysis of the Courts of the United States, England, and France. 2d ed., rev. & enl. New York: Oxford University Press, 1968. 496p. 68-18562 K63.A2 1968
A scholarly and balanced discussion of the judicial systems of the countries covered.

Murphy, Walter F. The Study of Public Law. With Joseph Tanenhaus. New York: Random House, 1972. 242p. 78-152856 KF4550.M85
Examines the elements of public law and the judicial process of the United States.

PUBLIC OPINION (POLLS, etc.)

Childs, Harwood L. Public Opinion; Nature, Formation, Role. Princeton, N.J.: Van Nostrand, 1965. 376p. 65-1358 HM261.C52
This study examines the development of public opinion and its effect upon society.

Devine, Donald J. The Political Culture of the United States; The Influence of Member Values on Regime Maintenance. Boston: Little, Brown, 1972. 383p. 70-177904 HN90.P8D48
Focuses on political socialization of citizens and the part public opionion plays on U.S. politics and government.

Gallup, George H. The Sophisticated Poll Watcher's
   Guide. Princeton, N. J. : Princeton Opinion Press,
   1972. 232p. 79-188499 HM261.G33
   A basic guide to public opinion polls by a pioneer in
   the field.

Lane, Robert Edwards. Public Opinion. With David O.
   Sears. Englewood Cliffs, N. J. : Prentice-Hall, 1964.
   120p. 64-13094 HM261.L2
   Analyzes the impact of public opinion in a democratic
   environment.

Luttbeg, Norman R. , comp. Public Opinion and Public
   Policy; Models of Political Linkage. Rev. ed. Home-
   wood, Ill. : Dorsey Press, 1974. 477p. 73-93358
   HM261.L85 1974
   A collection of readings on public opinion, political
   parties and their interrelationships.

Roll, Charles W. Polls: Their Use and Misuse in Politics. With Albert H. Cantril. New York: Basic
   Books, 1972. 177p. 72-86682 HM261.R58
   Emphasizes the misuse of polls in the electoral process within the United States.

Wilcox, Allen R. , comp. Public Opinion and Political
   Attitudes. New York: Wiley, 1974. 667p. 73-8945
   HN90.P8W5
   Each essay examines the process of attitude develop-
   ments related to political affairs and its effect upon
   public opinion.

REPRESENTATIVE GOVERNMENT AND REPRESENTATION

Birch, Anthony H. Representation. New York: Praeger,
   1972. 149p. 78-100911 JF1051.B55
   Discusses the conceptual aspects of representative
   government.

Pennock, James R. Representation. With John W. Chapman. New York: Atherton Press, 1968. 317p.
   68-16404 JF1051.P395
   The yearbook of the American Society for Political and
   Legal Philosophy. It focuses on U. S. forms of representation.

Pitkin, Hanna F. The Concept of Representation. Berkeley: University of California Press, 1967. 323p.
67-25052 JF1051.P5
Evaluates the theoretical constructs of representation
and traces their development.

REPUBLICAN PARTY

Burdette, Franklin L. The Republican Party; A Short
History. 2d ed. New York: Van Nostrand, 1972.
214p. 72-2352 JK2356.B94 1972
Reviews the historical development of the Republican
Party and many of its leaders.

Donovan, Robert J. The Future of the Republican Party.
New York: New American Library, 1964. 139p.
64-66377 E846.D6
Analyzes the future of Republicanism in U.S. party
politics.

Jones, Charles O. The Republican Party in American
Politics. New York: Macmillan, 1965. 153p.
65-15191 JK2356.J64
Discusses the general historical background of the Republican Party along with U.S. parties in general and
congressional leaders in particular.

Sherman, Richard B. The Republican Party and Black
America from McKinley to Hoover, 1896-1933.
Charlottesville: University Press of Virginia, 1973.
274p. 72-96714 JK2357.1896c.S53
Investigates the Republican Party's role in the suffrage
of Blacks in U.S. politics for the period covered.

REVOLUTIONS

Calvert, Peter. Revolution. New York: Praeger, 1970.
174p. 77-95664 JC491.C23
A conceptual analysis of revolutions in society.

_____. A Study of Revolution. Oxford: Clarendon
Press, 1970. 249p. 73-563588 JC491.C225
Develops the nature and causes of revolutions.

Greene, Thomas H.   Comparative Revolutionary Movements.   Englewood Cliffs, N.J.:   Prentice-Hall, 1974.
172p.   74-793   JC491.G67
Clearly explains the role of revolutions in the development of modern governments.

Kautsky, Karl.   Terrorism and Communism; A Contribu-
tion to the Natural History of Revolution.   Translated
by W. H. Kerridge.   Westport, Conn.:   Hyperion
Press, 1973.   234p.   73-844   HX36.K3   1973
A reprint of the 1920 edition which discusses the historical development of revolutions and Communism.

Lutz, William, comp.   On Revolution.   Edited with Harry
Brent.   Cambridge, Mass.:   Winthrop Publishers,
1971.   344p.   70-145761   JC491.L83
A collection of scholarly essays dealing with the role
of revolution and its political consequences.

Rejai, Mostafa.   The Strategy of Political Revolution.
Garden City, N.Y.:   Anchor Press, 1973.   189p.
70-182918   JC491.R44
A collection of case studies along with analysis of research.

Said, Abdul A.   Revolutionism.   With Daniel M. Collier.
Boston: Allyn and Bacon, 1971.   204p.   74-113085
JC491.S18
A general account of revolutionary activity within an
historical context.

ROUSSEAU, JEAN JACQUES

The Social Contract.   A classic of political thought.
Many editions are available.

RUSSIA   see   SOVIET UNION

SEPARATION OF POWERS

Bondy, William.   The Separation of Governmental Powers:
In History, in Theory, and in the Constitutions.   New
York: AMS Press, 1967.   185p.   79-29876
JK305.B68   1967

This study offers a clear view of this concept in U.S. politics and government.

Fisher, Louis. President and Congress; Power and Policy. New York: Free Press, 1972. 347p. 78-142362 JK305. F55
Describes and analyzes the different roles of the executive and legislative branches in American politics.

Hardin, Charles M. Presidential Power & Accountability; Toward a New Constitution. Chicago: University of Chicago Press, 1974. 257p. 73-92022 JK305. H37
Introduces the conflict between presidential power and the separation of powers doctrine.

Wilcox, Francis O. Congress, the Executive, and Foreign Policy. New York: Harper & Row, 1971. 179p. 74-160654 JK570. W55
Focuses on the foreign affairs aspects of the separation of powers concept.

SOCIALISM

Ader, Emile B. Socialism. Woodbury, N.Y.: Barron's Educational Series, Inc., 1966. 240p. 65-25683 HX36. A535
Details the history and development of socialism in the contemporary world.

Forman, James D. Socialism; Its Theoretical Roots and Present-Day Development. New York: Watts, 1972. 129p. 72-6736 HX36. F62
A brief theoretical analysis. Examines current applications in socialist nations.

Gorz, André. Socialism and Revolution. Translated by Norman Denny. Garden City, N.Y.: Anchor Books, 1973. 270p. 74-186054 HX44. G613
Outlines the revolutionary tendencies of socialism.

SOVEREIGNTY

Ionescu, Ghita. Between Sovereignty and Integration. New York: Wiley, 1974. 192p. 73-19586 JC327. I5 1974

A selection of readings on the problem of sovereignty and European federation.

Jessup, Philip C.   The Birth of Nations.   New York: Columbia University Press, 1974.   361p.   73-15515 JX1977. 2. A1J48
An expert examines the formation of new states and the role of the United Nations.

Klein, Robert A.   Sovereign Equality Among States: The History of an Idea.   Toronto: University of Toronto Press, 1974.   198p.   73-82582   JX4041. K57

Merriam, Charles E.   History of the Theory of Sovereignty Since Rousseau.   With a new introd. by Harold D. Lasswell.   New York: Garland Pub. , 1972. 233p.   78-147736   JC327. M5   1972
A classic treatment of the subject.   A reprint of the 1900 ed.

Nincic, Djura.   The Problem of Sovereignty in the Charter and in the Practice of the United Nations.   The Hague: M. Nijhoff, 1970.   358p.   76-574624   JX4041. N5413
Discusses the problems involved in the development of sovereignty among the members of the United Nations.

SOVIET UNION--POLITICS AND GOVERNMENT

Barghoorn, Frederick C.   Politics in the USSR; A Country Study.   2d ed.   Boston: Little, Brown, 1972. 360p.   72-4360   JN6531. B3   1972
Examines current Soviet politics and problems.

Hendel, Samuel, ed.   The Soviet Crucible; The Soviet System in Theory and Practice.   4th ed.   North Scituate, Mass. : Duxbury Press, 1973.   436p.   72-85269 JN6511. H4   1973
A basic text with additional coverage of economic conditions and Soviet politics.

Kanet, Roger E.   The Soviet Union and the Developing Nations.   Baltimore: Johns Hopkins University Press, 1974.   302p.   73-15530   DK274. K33
Assesses the Soviet Union's activities in the politics of new states.

Osborn, Robert J. The Evolution of Soviet Politics.
Homewood, Ill. : Dorsey Press, 1974. 574p. 73-
89118 JN6515. 1974. O83
An in-depth survey of Soviet politics and government.

Rositzke, Harry H. The USSR Today. New York: John
Day Co. , 1973. 114p. 72-2407 DK274. R624
A brief examination of political trends in contemporary
Russia.

Tucker, Robert C. The Soviet Political Mind; Stalinism
and Post-Stalin Change. Rev. ed. New York: Norton,
1971. 304p. 70-139391 DK274. T8 1971
An interpretative study of how Soviet political leaders
think and act.

Ulam, Adam B. The Russian Political System. New York:
Random House, 1974. 180p. 73-22494 JN6515 1917. U43
Provides a basic discussion of current Soviet politics.

Wesson, Robert G. The Soviet Russian State. New York:
Wiley, 1972. 404p. 70-39013 JN6515 1972. W47
Details the Soviet political system and its functions
within its Communist framework.

STATE, THE

Greaves, Harold R. G. The Foundations of Political
Theory. 2d ed. New York: Praeger, 1967. 208p.
67-12483 JC257. G7 1967a
Details the development of the state in political thought.

Krader, Lawrence. Formation of the State. Englewood
Cliffs, N. J. : Prentice-Hall, 1968. 118p. 68-10655
JC11. K73
An anthropological view of the state and its development
and foundations.

Laski, Harold J. Authority in the Modern State. Hamden, Conn. : Archon Books, 1968. 398p. 68-21685
JC327. L35 1968
A reprint of the 1919 ed. Examines the authoritarian
basis of the state and its role in political thought.

STATE GOVERNMENTS

Adrian, Charles R.   Governing Our Fifty States and Their
Communities.   3d ed.   New York: McGraw-Hill, 1972.
135p.   78-174608   JK2408.S28   1972
An overview of state and local government in the United
States.

American State and Local Government.   By Claudius O.
Johnson and others.   5th ed.   New York: Crowell,
1972.   307p.   73-187600   JK2408.A68   1972
A collection of readings examining various problems
and issues.

Dye, Thomas R.   Politics in States and Communities.
2d ed.   Englewood Cliffs, N.J.:   Prentice-Hall, 1973.
548p.   72-11912   JK2408.D82   1973
An in-depth survey of local politics and government in
the United States.

Halacy, Daniel S.   Government by the States; A History.
Indianapolis: Bobbs-Merrill, 1973.   205p.   72-88760
JK2408.H26
A brief historical survey of state government covering
basic structures.

Zimmerman, Joseph F.   State and Local Government.
2d ed.   New York: Barnes & Noble, 1970.   347p.
70-124363   JK2408.Z5   1970
A general outline and survey.

STATES, NEW

Alderfer, Harold F.   Public Administration in Newer Nations.   New York: Praeger, 1967.   206p.   68-14156
JF51.A56
A comparative study of the administrative problems of
new states.

Crises and Sequences in Political Development.   Contribu-
tions: Leonard Binder and others.   Princeton, N.J.:
Princeton University Press, 1971.   326p.   79-141952
JF60.C73
A collection of essays discussing the difficulties in the
political development of new nations.

More, Shankar S. Remodeling of Democracy for Afro-
Asian Nations. Westport, Conn.: Greenwood Press,
1973. 347p. 72-9810 JF60.M67 1973
Outlines political problems of the new Afro-Asian
states. A reprint of the 1962 ed.

Nwabueze, Benjamin O. Constitutionalism in the Emer-
gent States. Rutherford, N.J.: Fairleigh Dickinson
University Press, 1973. 316p. 72-14221 No LC
class. no. given.
A comparative analysis focusing on the constitutional
development of emerging nations.

TELEVISION IN POLITICS

Gilbert, Robert E. Television and Presidential Politics.
North Quincy, Mass.: Christopher Pub. House, 1972.
335p. 76-189366 HE8700.7.P6G5
Evaluates the impact of television coverage of presidential elections and its effect on public opinion.

Mickelson, Sig. The Electric Mirror: Politics in an Age
of Television. New York: Dodd, Mead, 1972. 304p.
74-39223 HE8700.7.P6N53
A critical review of television's role in political decision-making in the United States.

Minow, Newton N. Presidential Television. With John
Bartlow Martin and Lee M. Mitchell. New York:
Basic Books, 1973. 232p. 73-81134 HE8700.7.P6M57
Discusses the basic role of television as a tool of
presidents in influencing public opinion.

Wilhelmsen, Frederick D. Telepolitics; The Politics of
Neuronic Man. With Jane Bret. Plattsburgh, N.Y.:
Tundra Books, 1972. 254p. 73-187493 HE8700.7.
P6W57
Presents a psychological view of television's impact on
the average voter.

TOTALITARIANISM

Arendt, Hannah. The Origins of Totalitarianism. New
ed. New York: Harcourt Brace Jovanovich, 1973.
527p. 73-158194 JC481.A62 1973

An in-depth study of totalitarian thought and its historical development.

Chapman, Brian. Police State. New York: Praeger,
1970. 150p. 70-95665 JC481. C46
A brief theoretical view of totalitarianism and its origins.

Friedrich, Carl J. Totalitarianism in Perspective; Three
Views. With Michael Curtis and Benjamin R. Barber.
New York: Praeger, 1969. 164p. 78-76787 JC481. F75
A comparative analysis from three points of view.

Niemeyer, Gerhart. Between Nothingness and Paradise.
Baton Rouge: Louisiana State University Press, 1971.
226p. 74-139554 JC481. N52
Describes and analyzes the relationship of totalitarianism
and ideology.

Schapiro, Leonard B. Totalitarianism. New York:
Praeger, 1972. 144p. 76-100924 JC481. S35
Discusses the basis and development of totalitarianism
and modern political thought.

UNDERDEVELOPED AREAS--POLITICS

Clark, Robert P. Development and Instability: Political
Change in the Non-Western World. Hinsdale, Ill. :
Dryden Press, 1974. 279p. 73-83343 JF60. C55
Emphasizes the process of change in the politics of un-
derdeveloped areas.

Eisenstadt, Shomuel N. Traditional Patrimonialism and
Modern Neopatrimonialism. Beverly Hills, Calif. :
Sage Publications, 1973. 95p. 73-89066 JF60. E38
A theoretical study of the politics of developing areas
and their social conditions.

Finkle, Jason L. , ed. Political Development and Social
Change. Edited with Richard W. Gable. 2d ed. New
York: Wiley, 1971. 685p. 72-149769 JF60. F54
1971
These wide ranging essays cover social change in un-
derdeveloped areas along with political problems.

Heeger, Gerald A.   The Politics of Underdevelopment.
New York: St. Martin's Press, 1974.   150p.
73-91694   JF60.H43
A general exploration of politics in new states and underdeveloped areas.

Palmer, Monte.   The Dilemmas of Political Development;
An Introduction to the Politics of the Developing Areas.
Itasca, Ill.: F. E. Peacock Publishers, 1973.   213p.
72-89726   JF60.P34
Examines the factors determining the political structure
of developing nations.

Tsurutani, Taketsugu.   The Politics of National Development; Political Leadership in Transitional Societies.
New York: Chandler Pub. Co., 1973.   193p.
70-37749   JF251.T78
Focuses on the qualities of leadership in the politics of
new states.

Tullis, F. LaMond.   Politics and Social Change in Third
World Countries.   New York: Wiley, 1973.   372p.
72-10961   JF60.T85
Presents case studies in the politics and social transi-
tions of new states.

Uphoff, Norman T., comp.   The Political Economy of De-
velopment; Theoretical and Empirical Contributions.
Edited with Warren F. Ilchman.   Berkeley: Univer-
sity of California Press, 1972.   506p.   77-161999
JF60.U64
Essays on political issues of underdeveloped areas.
Focuses on economic developments and policies.

UNITED NATIONS

Barros, James.   The United Nations: Past, Present, and
Future.   New York: Free Press, 1972.   279p.
72-75159   JX1977.B317
Intended as introductory readings, these essays cover
the development of the United Nations and outline prospects for the future.

Chen, Samuel Shih-Tsai.   The Theory and Practice of International Organization.   2d ed.   New York: MSS Information Corp., 1973.   213p.   73-16019   JX1977.C496

1973
Discusses the relationship of theory and practice in the
United Nations in particular and international organiza-
tions in general.

Coyle, David C. The United Nations and How It Works.
Rev. ed. New York: New American Library, 1969.
256p.   71-5754   JX1977. C65   1969
A brief structural and developmental discussion of the
United Nations and its agencies.

Elmandjra, Mahdi. The United Nations System; An Analysis. Hamden, Conn.: Ardhon Books, 1973.   368p.
73-2840   JX1977. E46
Interprets the goals and objectives of the United Nations and analyzes its role in world politics.

Epstein, Edna. The United Nations. 8th rev. ed. New
York: Watts, 1973.   97p.   No LC card no. given.
JX1977. Z8E6   1973
Discusses the purpose and organization of the United
Nations and describes the work of its many specialized
agencies.

Goodrich, Leland M. The United Nations in a Changing
World. New York: Columbia University Press, 1974.
280p.   74-893   JX1977. G67
A sound and balanced appraisal of the United Nation's
role in world affairs.

Hazzard, Shirley. Defeat of an Ideal; A Study of the Self-
Destruction of the United Nations. Boston: Little,
Brown, 1973.   286p.   72-3783   JX1977. H38
A critical analysis of the United Nations and its fail-
ures in the international arena.

The United Nations: A Reassessment; Sanctions, Peace-
keeping, and Humanitarian Assistance. Edited by John
M. Paxman and George T. Boggs. Charlottesville:
University Press of Virginia, 1973.   153p.   73-86614
JX1977. U437
The proceedings of a symposium. The essays assess
the effect of the United Nations in world politics.

UNITED STATES.   CONGRESS.

American Assembly.   The Congress and America's Future.
David B. Truman, editor.   2d ed.   Englewood Cliffs,
N. J. :   Prentice-Hall, 1973.   216p.   72-10005
JK1061. A73   1973
These essays designed as background reading on the
role of the Congress in American politics, were given
at the American Assembly.

Congressional Quarterly, Inc.   Guide to the Congress of
the United States; Origins, History and Procedure.
Washington: Congressional Quarterly Service, 1971.
639, 323a, 21bp.   78-167743   JK1021. C56
A general survey and overview.

Harris, Joseph P.   Congress and the Legislative Process.
2d ed.   New York: McGraw-Hill, 1972.   192p.
78-172654   JK1061. H28   1972
Describes and analyzes the foundations of the American
legislative process and the role the Congress plays in
it.

Lowi, Theodore J. , comp.   Legislative Politics U. S. A.
Edited with Randall B. Ripley.   3d ed.   Boston: Little,
Brown, 1973.   383p.   73-9206   JK1061. L6   1973
A group of essays concerned with the impact of the
legislative function on American government and poli-
tics.

Matthews, Donald R.   U. S. Senators and Their World.
With a new introd.   New York: Norton, 1973.   303p.
73-9805   JK1161. M35   1973
A study of the Senate as an institution and the behavior
of its membership.

Redman, Eric.   The Dance of Legislation.   New York:
Simon and Schuster, 1973.   319p.   72-93515
KF4980. R4
Details the problems of getting legislation through the
Congress and focuses on the role of the Senate.

Rieselbach, Leroy N.   Congressional Politics.   New York:
McGraw-Hill, 1973.   426p.   72-5203   JK1061. R48
An in-depth study of the Congress, its structure and
processes.

UNITED STATES--CONSTITUTIONAL LAW

Bartholomew, Paul C.   Summaries of Leading Cases on
the Constitution.   8th ed.   Totowa, N.J. :   Littlefield,
Adams, 1972.   386p.   72-177511   KF4547. 8. B3   1972
Provides short summaries of outstanding Supreme
Court cases dealing with the development of the United
States Constitution.

Corwin, Edward S.   The Constitution and What It Means
Today.   Rev. by Harold W. Chase and Craig R. Ducat.
13th ed.   Princeton, N.J. :   Princeton University Press,
1973   601p.   72-7800   KF4550. C64   1973
A standard work on U. S. Constitutional law.

_____.   Corwin and Peltason's Understanding the Con-
stitution.   6th ed.   Hinsdale, Ill. :   Dryden Press,
1973.   228p.   73-613   KF4528. C67   1973
A basic outline of Constitutional law.

Pritchett, Charles H.   The American Constitutional System.   3d ed.   New York: McGraw-Hill, 1971.   149p.
76-141300   KF4550. Z9P7   1971
Examines the process of American Constitutional law
and the cases which developed its character.

UNITED STATES--FOREIGN RELATIONS

Armacost, Michael H.   The Foreign Relations of the
United States.   With Michael M. Stoddard.   2d ed.
Encino, Calif. :   Dickenson Pub. Co. , 1974.   243p.
74-79431   JX1705. A74   1974
Provides a historical survey of U. S. foreign affairs
since 1945.

Bloomfield, Lincoln P.   In Search of American Foreign
Policy; The Humane Use of Power.   New York: Ox-
ford University Press, 1974.   182p.   73-90342
JX1417. B56
Analyzes the present problems of American foreign
relations.

Cohen, Bernard C.   The Public's Impact on Foreign
Policy.   Boston: Little, Brown, 1973.   222p.
72-6872   JX1706. A4   1973

This study treats the effect of public opinion on America's foreign relations.

Coplin, William D. American Foreign Policy: An Introduction to Analysis and Evaluation. With Patrick J. McGowan and Michael K. O'Leary. North Scituate, Mass.: Duxbury Press, 1974. 272p. 73-80878 E744. C764
Provides a conceptual framework for analyzing the foreign relations of the U.S. and its administration.

Crabb, Cecil Van Meter. American Foreign Policy in the Nuclear Age. 3d ed. New York: Harper & Row, 1972. 528p. 71-168366 E744. C793 1972
A critical analysis of U.S. foreign relations and the administrative problems involved.

Halperin, Morton H. Bureaucratic Politics and Foreign Policy. With the assistance of Priscilla Clapp and Arnold Kanter. Washington: The Brookings Institution, 1974. 340p. 73-22384 JX1706. A4 1974
Related the significant aspects of foreign policy administration to the bureaucratic process in the U.S.

Merli, Frank J. Makers of American Diplomacy, from Benjamin Franklin to Henry Kissinger. Edited with Theodore A. Wilson. New York: Scribner, 1974. 728p. 73-1321 E183. 7. M472
A general survey of leading American statesmen and their role in shaping U.S. foreign policy.

Seabury, Paul. The United States in World Affairs. New York: McGraw-Hill, 1973. 124p. 72-4817 JX1407. S38
A readable account of U.S. involvement in world politics.

Spanier, John W. American Foreign Policy Since World War II. 6th ed. New York: Praeger, 1973. 305p. 72-91350 E744. S8 1973
A general study of U.S. involvement in world affairs since 1945. One of the better works on the subject.

_____. How American Foreign Policy Is Made. With Eric M. Uslaner. New York: Praeger, 1974. 180p. 73-8394 JX1706. A4 1974b

An analysis of the administration of American foreign relations.

Wellborn, Fred W.   Diplomatic History of the United States.   Totowa, N. J. : Littlefield, Adams, 1970. 458p.   76-19037   E183. 7. W46   1970
An outline account of U. S. foreign affairs.

UNITED STATES--POLITICS AND GOVERNMENT

Adrian, Charles R.   American Politics Reappraised; The Enchantment of Camelot Dispelled.   With Charles Press.   New York: McGraw-Hill, 1974.   326p. 73-11205   JK274. A5295
A critical analysis of the American political system.

Birnbach, Martin.   American Political Life; An Introduction to United States Government.   Homewood, Ill. : Dorsey Press, 1971.   590p.   75-149909   JK274. B58
A basic survey of American government for students.

Burns, James M.   Government by the People.   With J. W. Peltason.   8th ed.   Englewood Cliffs, N. J. : Prentice-Hall, 1972.   777p.   79-38778   JK274. B8525   1972
An introductory survey covering national, state, and local government in the U. S.

Davis, James W.   An Introduction to Public Administration; Politics, Policy, and Bureaucracy.   New York: Free Press, 1974.   336p.   73-16906   JK421. D36
Traces the role of the administrator in the executive function at the federal and local levels of government.

Dolbeare, Kenneth M.   American Politics; Policies, Power, and Change.   With Murray J. Edelman.   2d ed.   Lexington, Mass. : Heath, 1974.   568p.   73-3949 JK271. D62   1974
A basic survey and text focusing on political power and change.

Ferguson, John H.   The American System of Government. With Dean E. McHenry.   12th ed.   New York: McGraw-Hill, 1973.   801p.   73-770   JK274. F365 1973
Covers the foundation, structure and functions of American government and politics.

Hofferbert, Richard I. The Study of Public Policy. Indianapolis: Bobbs-Merrill, 1974. 275p. 73-9826
JK271. H7
A policy science approach to American political institutions.

Hofstadter, Richard. The American Political Tradition
and the Men Who Made It. With a foreword by Christopher Lasch. New York: Vintage Books, 1974. 501p.
73-20353 E178. H727 1974
A scholarly history of U. S. governmental institutions
from the viewpoint of the men who shaped it.

Liston, Robert A. Who Really Runs America? Garden
City, N. Y. : Doubleday, 1974. 207p. 73-11715
JK271. L537
Examines the control of power in the United States,
how and where it is exercised, and who is involved.

Litt, Edgar. Democracy's Ordeal in America: A Guide
to Political Theory and Action. Hinsdale, Ill. : Dryden
Press, 1973. 263p. 73-2796 JK271. L539
Deals with the economic and social policy in American
politics.

Livingston, John C. The Consent of the Governed. With
Robert G. Thompson. 3d ed. New York: Macmillan,
1971. 562p. 78-132455 JK271. L55 1971
Designed for students of American government and
theories of democracy, this extensive revised work
argues that there is a serious crisis in American poli-
tics--a crisis stemming from a gap between traditional
democratic ideals and American pluralistic political
practice.

Markun, Patricia M. Politics. Illus. by Ted Schroeder.
New York: Watts, 1970. 62p. 72-93221 JK271. M277
Analyzes the art of politics--what it is, who takes part,
lobbying, modern politics, dirty politics, and projec-
tions for the year 2000. Written especially for children.

Melville, J. Keith. The American Democratic System.
New York: Dodd, Mead, 1974. 353p. 73-15383
JK274. M526
A basic text and survey of the American political sys-
tem.

Patman, Wright.   Our American Government and How It
Works; 697 Questions and Answers.   7th ed.   New
York: Barnes & Noble, 1974.   210p.   73-9927
JK274. P344   1974
An outline of U. S. political institutions by a legislator.

Saye, Albert B.   Principles of American Government.
With Merritt B. Pound and John F. Allums.   7th ed.
Englewood Cliffs, N. J. :   Prentice-Hall, 1974.   390p.
73-17299   JK274. S38   1974
One of the outstanding basic texts in the field.

UNITED STATES.   SUPREME COURT

Abraham, Henry J.   The Judiciary; The Supreme Court
in the Governmental Process.   3d ed.   Boston: Allyn
and Bacon, 1973.   180p.   72-98005   KF8748. A2   1973
Discusses the role of the Supreme Court in American
politics.

_____.   Justices and Presidents; A Political History
of Appointments to the Supreme Court.   New York:
Oxford University Press, 1974.   310p.   73-90341
KF8742. A72
A thorough study of the presidential appointments of
Supreme Court justices.

Bickel, Alexander M.   The Supreme Court and the Idea
of Progress.   New York: Harper & Row, 1970.   210p.
74-20597   KF8748. B55   1970b
Develops the advancements of the Supreme Court over
the years.

Hyneman, Charles S.   The Supreme Court on Trial.
Westport, Conn. :   Greenwood Press, 1974.   308p.
73-20501   KF8748. H95   1974
An in-depth study of the problems of judicial review
and the Supreme Court.   A reprint of the 1963 ed.

McCloskey, Robert G.   The Modern Supreme Court.
Cambridge, Mass. :   Harvard University Press, 1972.
376p.   70-173408   KF8742. M3
A general history of the Supreme Court and its justices.

Spaeth, Harold J.   An Introduction to Supreme Court De-
cision Making.   Rev. and enl. ed.   San Francisco:
Chandler Pub. Co. , 1971. 87p.   78-171594
KF8748. S54   1972
Briefly describes the problem of judicial decision-
making and the Supreme Court.

Steamer, Robert J.   The Supreme Court: Constitutional
Revision and the New "Strict Constructionalism. "
Minneapolis: Burgess Pub. Co. , 1973. 35p.   72-92568
KF8748. S84
A brief outline of the issue of strict interpretation of
the Constitution by the Supreme Court.

Strum, Philippa.   The Supreme Court and "Political Ques-
tions": A Study in Judicial Evasion.   University:
University of Alabama Press, 1974.   188p.   73-13435
KF8748. S87
Seeks to define the precise role of the Supreme Court
in its decision related to highly politicized issues.

VOTING

Abrams, Robert.   Some Conceptual Problems of Voting
Theory.   Beverly Hills, Calif. : Sage Publications,
1973.   52p.   73-87847 JF1001. A25
A theoretical analysis of voting behavior.

Alford, Robert R.   Party and Society; The Anglo-American
Democracies.   Westport, Conn. : Greenwood Press,
1973.   396p.   72-9541 JF1001. A4   1973
A reprint of the 1963 ed. which discusses the sociological foundations of voting attitudes.

Farquharson, Robin.   Theory of Voting.   New Haven:
Yale University Press, 1969.   83p.   70-81417
JF1001. F33   1969
Constructs a model for voting analysis.

Flanigan, William H.   Political Behavior of the American
Electorate.   2d ed.   Boston: Allyn and Bacon, 1972.
143p.   73-158994 JK1967. F38   1972
A behavioral approach to voting habits and tendencies
of Americans.

Ku, Yü-ch'ang. Voting Procedures in International Politi-
cal Organizations. New York: Columbia University
Press; AMS Press, 1971. 349p. 79-137253
JX1995. K8 1971
Details the process of voting in international agencies
and the United Nations. A reprint of the 1947 ed.

WAR

Blainey, Geoffrey. The Causes of War. New York:
Free Press, 1973. 278p. 73-2016 U21. 2. B53 1973
Traces the basic causes of international conflict in
history.

Harrison, Robert. Warfare. Minneapolis, Minn. : Burgess Pub. Co. , 1973. 61p. 73-82852 U21. 2. H36
An anthropological approach to war in society.

Moore, Joseph T. War and War Prevention. With Ro-
berta Moore. Rochelle Park, N. J. : Hayden Book Co. ,
1974. 141p. 73-17107 JX1953. M76
Emphasizes the prevention of war in international relations.

Zabar, Simon. The White Flag Principle; How to Lose a
War and Why. New York: Simon and Schuster, 1973.
150p. 73-185342 U21. 2. Z26 1973
Considers the white flag principle and the causes as
well as consequences of international warfare.

WOMEN IN POLITICS

Chafe, William H. The American Woman; Her Changing
Social, Economic, and Political Roles, 1920-1970.
New York: Oxford University Press, 1972. 351p.
72-77496 HQ1426. C45
In part, this study deals with the political activities of
American women.

Chamberlin, Hope. A Minority of Members: Women in
the U. S. Congress. New York: Praeger Publishers,
1973. 374p. 73-151950 JK1030. A2C5
A biographical and historical directory of women active
in the Congress of the United States.

Jaquette, Jane S. , comp.   Women in Politics.   New York:
Wiley, 1974.   367p.   74-1037   HQ1236. J38
A collection of essays covering different aspects of
women's political activities in the United States.

Sanders, Marion K.   The Lady and the Vote.   Illustrated
by Charles E. Martin.   Westport, Conn. : Greenwood
Press, 1973.   172p.   73-13408   HQ1391. U5S3   1973
Outlines the struggle for women's suffrage in the United
States.   A reprint of the 1956 ed.

Chapter Four

SELECTED REFERENCE MATERIALS

Reference sources range from general works to knowledge of materials in other institutions that are not available
in one's own reference collection. Each reference source is
organized in a particular way to handle the special data it is
designed to convey. It comprises a carefully tended group
of information material, well designed, well edited, kept up
to date, conveniently arranged, and geared for constant use
in separate library quarters--namely, the reference room.
The use of reference volumes is almost second nature to expanding scholarship and the working core of a research center.

ABSTRACTS AND DIGESTS

Constitutional Law--United States

Bartholomew, Paul C. Summaries of Leading Cases on
the Constitution. 8th ed. Totowa, N.J.: Littlefield,
Adams, 1972. 386p. 72-177511
Provides short summaries of outstanding Supreme
Court cases dealing with the Constitution.

Political Parties--United States

Smith, Dwight L. The American Political Process; Se-
lected Abstracts of Periodical Literature, 1954-1971.
Edited with Lloyd W. Garrison. Santa Barbara,
Calif.: ABC-Clio Press, 1972. 630p. 72-77549
An extensive listing covering political parties, elections
and voting.

Political Science

International Political Science Abstracts. Oxford (Eng.):
  Blackwell, Paris: International Political Science Association, 1951+ v. 1+ 54-3623
  Includes 150 to 200 word abstracts of articles appearing
  in over 100 English and foreign language political science journals.

BIBLIOGRAPHIES

Africa--Politics

Alderfer, Harold F. A Bibliography of African Govern-
  ment, 1950-1966. 2d rev. ed. Lincoln, Pa.: Lincoln
  University Press, 1967. 163p. 67-27428
  An unannotated listing of books and articles on govern-
  ment, politics and public administration in Africa.
  Arranged by country, with an author index.

Asia, Southeastern

Tregonning, K. G. Southeast Asia: A Critical Bibliography. Tucson: University of Arizona Press, 1969.
  103p. 68-9845
  Includes over 2000 entries organized geographically by
  areas and country and subdivided topically.

Balkan Peninsula

Horecky, Paul L. Southeastern Europe; A Guide to Basic
  Publications. Chicago: University of Chicago Press,
  1969. 755p. 73-110336
  An annotated listing of materials relating to the states
  of southeastern Europe.

Books--Reviews

Gallup, Jennifer. Reference Guide to Reviews; A Check-
  list of Sources in the Humanities, Social Sciences, and
  Fine Arts. Vancouver: University of British Columbia Library, 1970. 38p. 79-588713
  Covers all of the basic reviewing media which include
  materials in the field of political science.

China (People's Republic of China, 1949-)--Foreign Re-
lations--Russia

Saran, Vimla. Sino-Soviet Schism, A Bibliography, 1956-
   1964. New York: Asia Pub. House, 1971. 162p.
   74-29951
   Covers Sino-Soviet relations in general and the schism
   in particular.

Civil Service Positions--United States

U. S. Civil Service Commission. Guide to Federal Career
   Literature. Washington: U. S. Gov. Print. Off. , 1971.
   28p.   70-616439
   A listing of materials on civil service jobs in the Federal government.

Communism

Bibliography on the Communist Problem in the United
   States. New York: Da Capo Press, 1971, c1955.
   474p.   71-169651
   A reprint of a basic bibliography.   However it is
   limited by the period of time covered.   It is primarily
   devoted to the literature relating to Communism in the
   United States since the birth, in 1919, of the first
   American parties adopting the Communist label.   The
   author index gives very brief descriptive annotations
   while the subject index arranges the same material in
   a topical outline.

Vigor, Peter H.   Books on Communism and the Communist Countries: A Selected Bibliography.   3d ed.
   London: Ampersand, 1971.   444p.   72-180508
   Lists both books and other materials on the development of Communism in various countries.

Community Power

Leif, Irving P.   Community Power and Decision-Making:
   An International Handbook.   Metuchen, N. J. : Scarecrow Press, 1974.   170p.   74-4171   Z7164. C842L43
   This handbook attempts to bring together all the research on community power in a useful reference format.   It lists books, journal articles, doctoral dissertations, master theses and papers presented at scholarly meetings.   Some 1196 items are included in a

subject arrangement, with complete citations and selective annotations.

County Government--United States

Bollens, John C.   American County Government, with an
Annotated Bibliography.   With John R. Bayes and
Kathryn L. Utter.   Beverly Hills, Calif.:   Sage Pub-
lications, 1969.   433p.   69-20118
Part 3 is a bibliographical essay on county government.
Has an author and title index.

Diplomacy

Harmon, Robert B.   The Art and Practice of Diplomacy:
A Selected and Annotated Guide.   Metuchen, N.J.:
Scarecrow Press, 1971.   355p.   75-142234 JX1662. H273
Lists and annotated 900 books, articles and pamphlets
on all phases of diplomacy.   Includes a glossary of
diplomatic terms and illustrative documents.

Moussa, Farag.   Diplomatie Contemporaine: Guide Bibli-
ographique.   2d ed.   Geneva: Carnegie Endowment
for International Peace, 1965.   201p.
An annotated bibliography of books, articles, pamphlets,
and dissertations pertaining to contemporary diplomacy
in all parts of the world.

Disarmament

Arms Control & Disarmament.   Washington: U.S. Gov.
Print. Off., 1964/65+   v. 1+   64-62746   JX1974. A1A7
Each issue has abstracts of recent books, articles and
other materials on the political, strategic, historical
and other aspects of arms control.

Drug Abuse

Wells, Dorothy P.   Drug Education; A Bibliography of
Available Inexpensive Materials.   Metuchen, N.J.:
Scarecrow Press, 1972.   111p.   72-317   Z7164. N17W45
Includes 400 items covering all aspects of the subject.
Brief annotations are given.

Elections--United States

Agranoff, Robert.   Elections and Electoral Behavior: A
Bibliography.   DeKalb: Center for Governmental

Studies, Northern Illinois University, 1972.   30ℓ.
72-189162   Z7165. U5A64
An unannotated bibliography of over 200 items on U. S.
electorial politics.

Kaid, Lynda L.   Political Campaign Communication: A
Bibliography and Guide to the Literature.   With Keith
R. Sanders and Robert O. Hirsch.   Metuchen, N. J.:
Scarecrow Press, 1974.   206p.   73-22492
Z7165. U5K34
Includes more than 1500 indexed citations to descrip-
tive, analytical, evaluative and experimental works on
the role and effects of communication in political cam-
paigns.

Europe, Eastern

Horecky, Paul L.   East Central Europe; A Guide to Basic
Publications.   Chicago: University of Chicago Press,
1969.   956p.   70-79472   Z2483. H56
An annotated listing of materials relating to the states
of East Central Europe.

Federal Government--United States

Stenberg, Carl W.   American Intergovernmental Relations;
A Selected Bibliography.   Monticello, Ill.: Council of
Planning Librarians, 1971.   37ℓ.   72-187195
Z5942. C68   no. 227
A brief listing of materials on intergovernmental prob-
lems in the United States.

Hague.   Permanent Court of International Justice

Douma, J. , comp.   Bibliography on the International
Court Including the Permanent Court, 1918-1964.
Leyden: A. W. Sijthoff, 1966.   387p.   No. LC number
An unannotated bibliography of over 3500 books, docu-
ments, and articles of the work, jurisdiction, and
cases of the League of Nations Permanent Court of
International Justice and the present U. N. International
Court of Justice.

Imperialism

Harmon, Robert B.   Imperialism as a Concept of Political Science: Essay and Bibliography.   San Jose,

Calif. : Bibliographic Information Center for the Study
of Political Science, 1971.   6p.   72-192540   JC359.H28
A brief study and unannotated bibliography on the conceptual aspects of imperialism.

International Law

Robinson, Jacob.   International Law and Organization.
General Sources of Information.   Leiden: A. W.
Sijthoff, 1967.   560p.   67-25746   Z6466.R6
An annotated bibliography of over 2000 sources of in-
formation on public international law and international
organization.

International Law--History--China (People's Republic of
China, 1949-)

Ho, Paul.   The People's Republic of China and Interna-
tional Law; A Selective Bibliography of Chinese Sources.
Washington: Far Eastern Law Division, Law Library,
Library of Congress, 1972.   45p.   72-5365
Z6465.C6H6
Includes items on the international aspects of Commu-
nist China's foreign relations.

International Offenses

Schutter, Bart de.   Bibliography on International Criminal
Law.   With the collaboration of Christian Eliaerts.
Leiden: A. W. Sijthoff, 1972.   423p.   72-80997
Z6464.C8S38
An extensive listing on international offenses and crimi-
nal jurisdiction.

International Organization

Johnson, Harold S.   International Organization; A Classified Bibliography.   With Baljit Singh.   East Lansing,
Mich. : Asian Studies Center, Michigan State University, 1969.   261p.   79-630542   Z6461.J63
An unannotated listing of over 4000 entries classified
under broad subject headings.

International Relations

Foreign Affairs Bibliography; A Selected and Annotated
List of Books on International Relations.   New York:

Russell & Russell, 1919-1932; R. R. Bowker, 1932-
1942; 1942-1952; 1952-1962. 4v. 60-11311
Lists books only, with brief annotations, but is the
most extensive bibliography in this area.

The Foreign Affairs 50-Year Bibliography; New Evaluations of Significant Books on International Relations
1920-1970. Byron Dexter, editor, assisted by Eliza-
beth H. Bryant and Janice L. Murray. New York:
Published for the Council on Foreign Relations by R.
R. Bowker Co., 1972. 936p. 75-163904 Z6461.F62
An annotated bibliography covering this extensive period. Includes the more important works on international relations.

U.S. Library of Congress. General Reference and Bib-
liography Division. A Guide to Bibliographic Tools for
Research in Foreign Affairs. Compiled by Helen F.
Conover. 2d ed. with supplement. Westport, Conn.:
Greenwood Press, 1970. 145, 15p. 68-55129
Z6461.U49 1970
An annotated listing of major bibliographies, manuals,
indexes, etc. in the field. A reprint of the 1958 ed.

Zawodny, Janusz K. Guide to the Study of International
Relations. San Francisco: Chandler Pub. Co., 1966.
151p. 65-16765 Z6461.Z3
A selected list and description of the more important
reference sources for the study of international relations. Arranged by type of material with subject and
title indexes.

Jurisprudence

Dias, Reginald W. M. A Bibliography of Jurisprudence.
2d ed. London: Butterworths, 1970. 445p.
72-579792 No class. given.
The most extensive single bibliography in this area.
A companion volume to his Jurisprudence, 2d ed.

Justice, Administration of

Zarefsky, David. Complete Handbook on the Administration of Justice; A Reference Manual for De-
baters and Others Interested in the Subject. With
Thomas B. McClain and Douglas Andrews. Skokie,
Ill.: National Textbook Co., 1971. 316p. 79-165768

KF8700. A1Z36
Arranged under broad topics, this is the most extensive
single bibliography on this subject.

Law--United States

Andrews, Joseph L. The Law in the United States of
America; A Selective Bibliographical Guide. With
others. New York: New York University Press, 1966.
100p. 67-1256 KF1. Z9A65 1966
A selected and annotated list of American legal materials. Provides an introduction to the basic publications under subject and form headings.

Harvard University. Law School. Library. Annual Legal Bibliography. Cambridge, Mass.: 1960/61+
v. 1+ 61-18217 K20. A1H3
An annual cumulation of selected books and articles ac-
quired by the Harvard University Law School Library.

Mersky, Roy M. Law Books for Non-Law Libraries and
Laymen; A Bibliography. Dobbs Ferry, N.Y.: Oceana
Publications, 1969. 110p. 69-15494 KF1. M4
Includes a condensed introduction to the intricacies and
instrumentalities of legal research.

Surrency, Erwin C. A Guide to Legal Research. With
Benjamin Feld, and Joseph Crea. Supplemented ed.
Dobbs Ferry, N.Y.: Oceana Publications, 1966.
128p. 67-1406 KF240. S8 1966.
Describes the methods of legal research in federal law,
federal administrative law, state statutory law and
state decisional law.

Law Enforcement

Prostano, Emanuel T. Law Enforcement; A Selective
Bibliography. With Martin L. Piccirillo. Littleton,
Colo.: Libraries Unlimited, 1974. 203p. 73-86399
27164. P76P74
This bibliography lists 1764 selected publications related to law enforcement. Intended as a guide not
only for those who function at an operational level but
also for institutions that offer instruction in its varying divisions.

League of Nations

Aufricht, Hans.   Guide to League of Nations Publications;
    A Bibliographical Survey of the Work of the League,
    1920-1947.   New York: AMS Press, 1966.   682p.
    73-161711   Z6473.A85   1966
    Describes fully the bibliographical apparatus available
    for the use of League of Nations publications.

Metropolitan Government--United States

White, Anthony G.   A Selected Bibliography: City-County
    Consolidation in the United States.   Monticello, Ill.:
    Council of Planning Librarians, 1972.   53p.   72-188918
    Z5942.C68   no. 294
    A basic listing of items covering various metropolitan
    governmental problems.

Mississippi Freedom Democratic Party

McDowell, Jennifer.   Black Politics: A Study and Anno-
    tated Bibliography of the Mississippi Freedom Demo-
    cratic Party.   With Milton Loventhal.   San Jose,
    Calif.:   Bibliographic Information Center for the Study
    of Political Science, 1971.   96p.   68-58320
    Z7161.B5515   no. 3
    An extensive study and annotated bibliography on the
    first major Black political party in America.

Military Art and Science--Dictionaries

Craig, Hardin.   A Bibliography of Encyclopedias and Dic-
    tionaries Dealing with Military, Naval, and Maritime
    Affairs, 1577-1971.   4th ed. rev. & corr.   Houston,
    Tex.:   Dept. of History, Rice University, 1971.   134p.
    72-189999   Z6724.D5C7   1971
    A basic bibliographical listing of dictionaries in this
    area with annotations.

Municipal Government

Brooks, Robert C.   A Bibliography of Municipal Problems
    and City Conditions.   New York: Arno Press, 1970.
    346p.   78-112527   Z7164.L8B9   1970
    An extensive coverage on cities and towns in general
    as well as municipal governments and urban problems.

Government Affairs Foundation. Metropolitan Communities: A Bibliography with Special Emphasis Upon Government and Politics. Chicago: Public Administration
Service, 1957. 392p. Supplement, 1957+
A series of volumes containing many references to bibliographies, books, articles, pamphlets, surveys, and
other materials, many annotated, on all aspects of
metropolitan government.

Nationalism

Deutsch, Karl W. Nationalism and National Development;
An Interdisciplinary Bibliography. With Richard L.
Merritt. Cambridge, Mass. : MIT Press, 1970.
519p. 79-90750 27164. N2D43
An unannotated listing of around 5000 books and articles
published on nationalism between 1935 and 1966.

Political Parties--United States

Jones, Charles O. The Role of Political Parties in Con-
gress; A Bibliography and Research Guide. With
Randall B. Ripley. Tucson: Published for the Insti-
tute of Government Research by the University of Ari-
zona Press, 1966. 41p. 66-63498 Z7165. U5J6
A listing of books and articles, with sections on Gene-
ral Works, Congressional Organization and Procedure,
Party Organization and Procedure, Party Leadership,
Party Voting and Methodology, Congressional Elections,
Constituency and Congress.

Wynar, Lubomyr R. American Political Parties; A Selective Guide to Parties and Movements of the 20th
Century. Littleton, Colo. : Libraries Unlimited, 1969.
427p. 75-96954 Z7165. U5W88
A bibliography of over 3000 titles on American political parties and their development in the current century.

Political Science

ABC Pol Sci; Advance Bibliography of Contents: Political
Science and Government. Santa Barbara, Calif. : ABC-
Clio Press, 1969+ v. 1+ 70-6512 27161. A214
Reproduces the tables of contents of about 260 journals
in political science, public administration, law and re-
lated fields.

A Bibliography for Students of Politics. London: Oxford
  University Press, 1971 113p. 70-25462 Z7161.B5526
  An unannotated listing of over 3000 items covering all
  fields of politics arranged under broad subject areas.

Brock, Clifton. The Literature of Political Science; A
  Guide for Students, Librarians, and Teachers. New
  York: Bowker, 1969. 232p. 79-79426 Z7161.B83
  Lists and describes the major sources of information
  in the field. Also a good general guide to the conduct
  of elementary research.

Harmon, Robert B. Political Science; A Bibliographical
  Guide to the Literature. Metuchen, N.J.: Scarecrow
  Press, 1965-74. 4v. 65-13557 Z7161.H27
  An extensive and partially annotated bibliography of
  political science materials including many in foreign
  languages.

Harvard University. Library. Government: Classification Schedule, Classified Listing by Call Number, Author and Title Listing, Chronological Listing. Cambridge, Mass., 1969 (dist. by Harvard University
  Press). 263p. 68-8886 Z7161.H284
  A classified list of books related to political science in
  the Widener Library at Harvard University.

Holler, Frederick L. The Information Sources of Political Science. 2d ed. Santa Barbara, Calif.: ABC-
  Clio Press, 1975. 5v. Z7161.H64 1974
  An annotated bibliography and guide to over 1000 reference sources essential to the study of political science.

International Bibliography of Political Science. Paris:
  UNESCO, Chicago: Aldine, 1953+ v. 1+ 54-14355
  Z163.I62
  A classified index to articles appearing in over 1000
  periodicals. Covers all the major and many minor political science journals. This annual bibliography lists
  major books, articles, pamphlets and other printed
  sources. It is arranged topically, with author and subject indexes, and provides an extensive source of material for research.

Kalvelage, Carl. Research Guide for Undergraduates in
  Political Science. With Morley Segal and Peter J. Anderson. Morristown, N.J.: General Learning Press,

1972. 140p.   78-185110
A general guide to research in political science. Includes most of the major sources of information in the
field, with some annotations.

Pogány, Andrås H.   Political Science and International
Relations; Books Recommended for the Use of Ameri-
can Catholic College and University Libraries.   With
Hortenzia L. Pogány.   Metuchen, N.J.:   Scarecrow
Press, 1967.   387p.   67-10196   Z7161.P58
An unannotated bibliography of over 5800 books.   Is in-
tended as a book selection guide for Catholic libraries.

Universal Reference System.   Political Science, Government & Public Policy Series.   Princeton, N.J.:
Princeton Research Pub. Co., 1965-69-   78-6367
Z6461.U66
A series of computer-produced bibliographies.   Index
covers ten sub-fields of political science.   Each volume
is updated by Quarterly Gazettes with annual cumulations.

Political Science--Methodology

Harmon, Robert B.   Methodology and Research in Political Science: An Annotated Bibliography.   San Jose,
Calif.:   Bibliographic Information Center for the Study
of Political Science, 1972.   15p.   72-188356
Z7161.B5515 no. 4
An annotated bibliography of books.   Includes a section
on compiling a bibliography.

Presidents--United States--Succession

Tompkins, Dorothy L.C.C.   Presidential Succession; A
Bibliography.   Rev.   Berkeley: Institute of Government
Studies, University of California, 1965.   29p.
66-63309   Z1249.P7T63   1965
A short bibliography of about 100 articles, books, and
documents on the problems of presidential disability
and succession.

Public Administration

California.   University.   Institute of Governmental Studies.
Research & Service: A Fifty Year Record.   Compiled
by Dorothy C. Tompkins.   Berkeley: University of

California, 1971.   154p.   77-169911   Z7164.A2C35
A catalog of publications relating to public administration, California politics, and U.S. Politics and Government.

Harmon, Robert B.   Basic Source Materials in Public Administration.   Monticello, Ill.:   Council of Planning Librarians, 1974.   12p.   No. LC card no. or class.
A brief list of the more important source materials in the field.   Includes annotations.

McCurdy, Howard E.   Public Administration: A Bibliography.   Washington, D.C.:   School of Government and Public Administration, American University, 1972.
156p.   72-169084   Z7164.A2M3
This bibliography contains 1000 books which are recognized as important in the discipline of public administration.   All of the titles in Part I are well annotated.

Spitz, Allan A.   Developmental Change; An Annotated Bibliography.   Lexington: University Press of Kentucky, 1969.   316p.   69-19766   Z7164.E15S615
Annotated listing of materials relating to economic development and public administration in underdeveloped areas.

Public Opinion

Childs, Harwood L.   A Reference Guide to the Study of Public Opinion.   Ann Arbor, Mich.:   Gryphon Books, 1971.   105p.   72-152249   Z7204.S67C5   1971
Contains a variety of useful bibliographies but without the aid of annotations.   Out of date but still useful.
A facsimilie reprint of the 1934 edition.

Social Indicators

Social Indicators and Societal Monitoring; An Annotated Bibliography.   By Leslie D. Wilcox and others.   San Francisco: Jossey-Bass, 1972.   464p.   74-154452
Z7164.S66S53   1972
Arranged by broad subjects this work provides an extensive annotated source for social data.

Social Sciences

Clarke, Jack Alden.   Research Materials in the Social Sciences.   2d ed.   Madison: University of Wisconsin

Press, 1957. 56p. 67-25948 Z7161.C56 1967
An annotated bibliography of 215 major reference materials in various social science fields.

Hoselitz, Berthold F., ed. A Reader's Guide to the Social Sciences. Rev. ed. New York: Free Press,
1970. 425p. 71-15373
A general introduction to the literature of the social
sciences. Although not specifically a bibliography,
this work describes the type of literature in each field
and cites the more important "classics" and their con-
tribution to the development of knowledge in respective
fields of specialization.

Mason, John B. Research Resources; Annotated Guide to
the Social Sciences. Santa Barbara, Calif.: ABC-Clio
Press, 1968+   68-9685 A7161.M36
An extensive and annotated listing of reference materials, periodicals, etc. in the social sciences.

White, Carl M., ed. Sources of Information in the Social
Sciences, A Guide to the Literature. With others.
2d ed. Chicago: American Library Association, 1973.
702p. 73-9825 Z7161.W49 1973
Intended as a selection tool for collection development
and as a handbook for reference librarians, scholars,
and students. Has chapters in each area prepared by
subject and reference specialists and includes many
cross references.

Wynar, Lubomyr R. Guide to Reference Materials in Po-
litical Science. With the assistance of Linda Fystrom.
Denver: Colorado Bibliographic Institute, Rochester,
N.Y.: Libraries Unlimited, 1966-68. 2v. 66-1321
Z7161.W9
Includes general and reference materials, but with
somewhat more emphasis on reference sources. An-
notates only major works.

Social Science--Bibliography--Theory, Methods, etc.

Boehm, Eric H. Blueprint for Bibliography; A System
for the Social Sciences and Humanities. Santa Barbara,
Calif.: Clio Press, 1965. 22p. 65-25556 Z1001.B66
An outline of automated methods in bibliographic practice in the social sciences and humanities.

Freides, Thelma K.   Literature and Bibliography of the
   Social Sciences.   Los Angeles: Melville Pub. Co. ,
   1973.   284p.   73-10111   H61. F635
   An excellent introduction to the literature and bibliography of the social sciences and problems in the field.

Sociological Jurisprudence

Chambliss, William J.   Sociology of the Law: A Research
   Bibliography.   With Robert B. Seidman.   Berkeley,
   Calif. : Glendessary Press, 1970.   113p.   73-140068
   KF1. C45
   A good listing of materials on sociological jurispru-
   dence and law in the United States.

Space Law

White, Irvin L.   Law and Politics in Outer Space; A Bibliography.   With Clifton E. Wilson and John A. Vos-
   burgh.   Tucson: University of Arizona Press, 1972.
   176p.   78-163011   JX5810. W53
   Covers books and articles in a broad subject arrangement.

United Nations

Brimmer, Brenda.   A Guide to the Use of United Nations
   Documents, Including Reference to the Specialized
   Agencies and Special U. N. Bodies.   With others.
   Dobbs Ferry, N. Y. : Oceana Publications, 1962.   272p.
   61-14550   Z674. N47   no. 3
   Contains detailed information on how to locate and use
   United Nations documents and publications.

McConaughy, John B.   A Student's Guide to United Nations
   Documents and Their Use.   With Hazel J. Blanks.
   New York: Council on International Relations and
   United Nations Affairs, 1969.   17p.   75-11872
   Z6481. M3
   A short guide to the steps required in locating and
   using U. N. documents.

Rothman, Marie H.   Citation Rules and Forms for United
   Nations Documents and Publications.   Brooklyn, N. Y. :
   Long Island University Press, 1971.   64p.   76-175484
   Z6481. A2R66
   Although covering mainly the rule for the citation of

U. N. documents it includes a listing of United Nations publications.

Winton, Harry N. M.   Publications of the United Nations System: A Reference Guide.   New York: R. R. Bowker, 1972.   202p.   72-1923   Z6481. W55
An extensive guide to U. N. publications and other international agencies.

United States--Executive Departments--Directories

Wynkoop, Sally.   Directories of Government Agencies. Compiled with David W. Parish.   Rochester, N. Y. : Libraries Unlimited, 1969.   242p.   70-84652 Z7165. U5W9
An annotated listing of directories of U. S. executive departments and other governmental agencies.

United States--Government Publications

Government Reference Books.   Littleton, Colo. : Libraries Unlimited, 1968/69+   v. 1+   76-146307   Z1223. 27G68
A biennial reviewing service describing reference titles published by the United States government and its agencies.

Pohle, Linda C.   A Guide to Popular Government Publications for Libraries & Home Reference.   Littleton, Colo. : Libraries Unlimited, 1972.   213p.   70-189256 Z1223. 27P63
Lists and describes 2000 government publications covering over 100 subjects.   Provides instructions for obtaining government publications.   Indexed by subject.

Poore, Benjamin P.   A Descriptive Catalogue of the Government Publications of the United States, September 5, 1774-March 4, 1881.   Washington: Gov. Print. Off. , 1885; New York: Johnson Reprint Corp, 1970. 2v.   74-29060   Z1223. A   1885d
A reprint of this valuable source of U. S. government documents from 1774 to 1881.

Wynkoop, Sally.   Subject Guide to Government Reference Books.   Littleton, Colo. : Libraries Unlimited, 1972. 276p.   72-83382   Z1223. Z7W95
Describes over 1000 reference books.   Material is arranged under broad subject categories, each of which

is further sub-divided by specific subjects in alphabetical order.

United States--Government Publications (State Governments)

Parish, David W.   State Government Reference Publications: An Annotated Bibliography.   Littleton, Colo. : Libraries Unlimited, 1974.   237p.   74-81322 Z1223. 5. A1P37
This is a selective, annotated guide to more than 800 important and representative documents issued by the offices and agencies of various states and U. S. territories.

United States--Politics and Government

Connery, Robert H.   Reading Guide in Politics and Government.   With Richard H. Leach and Joseph Zikmund II.   Washington, D. C. : National Council for the Social Studies, 1966.   85p.   66-26280   Z7165. U5C653
An annotated list of important books on American and comparative government and politics.

Urbanization--United States

Isika, Daniel.   Urban Growth Policy in the United States; A Bibliographic Guide.   Monticello, Ill. :   Council of Planning Librarians, 1972.   34p.   72-191344   Z5942. C68 no. 273
Includes items on urban problems and the growth of metropolitan areas.

World Politics

Foreign Relations Library.   Catalog of the Foreign Relations Library.   Boston: G. K. Hall, 1969.   9v.   75-6133   Z6209. F656
An extensive retrospective catalog covering all areas in international affairs.

BIBLIOGRAPHIES OF BIBLIOGRAPHIES

International Relations

Boehm, Eric H. , ed.   Bibliographies on International Relations and World Affairs; An Annotated Directory.

Santa Barbara, Calif. : Clio Press, 1965.   33p.
65-25555   Z1002. B65
Includes a list of the top twenty bibliographies related
to international relations based on the quantity of titles
listed.   Also contains an annotated directory of 83 publications with regular bibliographic listings.

Law

Besterman, Theodore.   Law & International Law; A Bibliography of Bibliographies.   Totowa, N. J. :   Rowman
and Littlefield, 1971.   436p.   72-178009   No LC Card
No.
An extensive unannotated listing covering both law in
general as well as international law.

Political Science

Harmon, Robert B.   Political Science Bibliographies.
Metuchen, N. J. :   Scarecrow Press, 1973+   v. 1+
72-8849   Z7161. A1H35.   V. 2, 1976.
A partially annotated listing of bibliographies.   Is international in scope and coverage.

DICTIONARIES

Cities and Towns

Abrams, Charles.   The Language of Cities; A Glossary
of Terms.   With the assistance of Robert Kolodny.
New York: Viking Press, 1971.   365p.   76-137500
HT108. 5. A24
Includes terms related to municipal government.

Communism

Hyams, Edward S.   A Dictionary of Modern Revolution.
New York: Taplinger Pub. Co. , 1973.   322p.   73-6175
HX17. H9   1973
A guide to modern radical movements.   Provides an
alphabetical listing of philosophies, ideologies, organizations, events and persons prominent in nineteenth
and twentieth century economic, political and social
movements.

International Relations

Haensch, Günther. Dictionary of International Relations
and Politics. Compiled with the cooperation of Adrien
R. de Clery, A. Canto and Fritz Koller. New York:
Elsevier Pub. Co. , 1965. 638p. 64-8710 JX1226. H26
Gives definitions and word equivalents in English,
French, German and Spanish of over 5000 terms re-
lated to international relations.

Plano, Jack C. The International Relations Dictionary.
With Roy Olton. New York: Holt, Rinehart and Winston, 1969. 337p. 69-17657 JX1226. P55
Defines terms and their significance. Definitions are
arranged under twelve broad subject headings. Has an
index of terms, etc.

Law

Black, Henry C. Black's Law Dictionary; Definitions of
the Terms and Phrases of American and English Jurisprudence, Ancient and Modern. Rev. 4th ed. St.
Paul, Minn. : West Pub. Co. , 1970. 1882p. 70-16796
KF156. B53 1970
An extensive dictionary of definitions to the terms,
phrases and maxims used in Anglo-American jurisprudence.

Military Art and Science

Luttwak, Edward. A Dictionary of Modern War. New
York: Harper & Row, 1971. 224p. 77-159574
U24. L93 1971
Covers the basic terms related to all aspects of mili-
tary science.

Quick, John. Dictionary of Weapons and Military Terms.
New York: McGraw-Hill, 1973. 515p. 73-8757
U24. Q5
An illustrated dictionary of terms and phrases related
to weapons and many kinds of martial arts.

Near East--Politics

Shimoni, Yaacov. Political Dictionary of the Middle East
in the Twentieth Century. Edited with E. Levine.
London: Weidenfeld and Nicolson, 1972. 434p.

72-188540   DS61. S52
Contains definitions of terms relating to the politics
and governments of the Middle East.

Political Science

Davis, Robert R.   Lexicon of Historical & Political Terms.
New York: Simon and Schuster, 1973.   133p.
74-151005   JA61. D36
Provides a carefully selected listing to the specialized
vocabulary used by historians and political scientists.
Each listing, alphabetically arranged, not only gives the
definition of the terms, but also includes a discussion
of its historical, political and social background.   Each
entry also has suggestions for in-depth reading in relevant areas.

Dunner, Joseph, ed.   Dictionary of Political Science.
Totowa, N. J. :   Littlefield, Adams, 1970, c1964.   585p.
NUC70-100188   JA61. D8   1970
An extensive description of terms related to political
science plus descriptive information about old and new
nations, former and contemporary statesmen and politicians.

Heimanson, Rudolph.   Dictionary of Political Science and
Law.   Dobbs Ferry, N. Y. :   Oceana Publications, 1967.
188p.   67-14401   JA61. H4
Covers terminology which related both to political science and law in general.

Plano, Jack C.   Dictionary of Political Analysis.   With
Robert E. Riggs.   Hinsdale, Ill. :   Dryden Press,
1973.   114p.   72-76942   JA61. P57
This dictionary defines and discusses several hundred
terms commonly used in the literature of modern political analysis.

Roberts, Geoffrey K.   A Dictionary of Political Analysis.
New York: St. Martin's Press, 1971.   229p.
70-151309   JA61. R62   1971b
Attempts to provide a concise but comprehensive dictionary of the terminology of political analysis, indicating where appropriate the major sources in which
the terms are used.

Social Sciences

Gould, Julius, ed.   A Dictionary of the Social Sciences.
    With William L. Kolb.   New York: Free Press of
    Glencoe, 1964.   761p.   64-20307   H41.G6
    Contains a wide coverage of terms and their meanings
    by many individual scholars.   Most entries are in the
    form of brief essays and includes numerous cross-
    references.

Zadrozny, John T.   Dictionary of Social Science.   Wash-
    ington: Public Affairs Press, 1959.   367p.   58-13401
    Contains only brief definitions of terms used in the so-
    cial sciences.

United States--Politics and Government

Holt, Solomon.   Dictionary of American Government.
    Rev. ed.   New York: Mcfadden-Bartell Corp., 1970.
    304p.   72-17208   JK9.H6   1970
    A popular dictionary containing over 1000 definitions
    of political terms, legal acts, Supreme Court decisions,
    etc.

Plano, Jack C.   The American Political Dictionary.   With
    Milton Greenberg.   3d ed.   Hinsdale, Ill.:   Dryden
    Press, 1972.   462p.   72-75601   JK9.P55   1972
    This comprehensive dictionary contains approximately
    1200 terms, concepts, Supreme Court cases, statutes,
    agencies, theories, and political ideas that relate to
    the American system of government and politics.

Safire, William L.   The New Language of Politics; A
    Dictionary of Catchwords, Slogans, and Political Usage.
    Rev. & enl.   New York: Collier Books, 1972.   782p.
    70-187800   JK9.S2   1972
    Entries consist of brief definitions followed by a fre-
    quently detailed description of the usage employed by
    politicians for the purpose of leading or misleading the
    public.

Smith Edward, C., ed.   Dictionary of American Politics.
    With Arnold J. Zurcher.   2d ed.   New York: Barnes
    & Noble, 1968.   434p.   67-28530   JK9.S5   1968
    Includes almost 4000 definitions of terms, slogans,
    nicknames, governmental agencies, legal acts, Supreme
    Court decisions and political concepts.

World Politics

Elliott, Florence. A Dictionary of Politics. 6th ed.
Baltimore: Penguin, 1971. 480p. 72-186214
D419.E4 1971
Contains entries for individual states, political parties,
organizations, living politicians and statesmen, and
some political terms.

Laqueur, Walter Z. A Dictionary of Politics. With the
assistance of Evelyn Anderson and others. Rev. ed.
New York: Free Press, 1974. 576p. 74-9232
D419.L36 1974b
This newly revised edition spans the past forty years
of events and personalities. More than 3000 entries
cover all the major nations, areas, and alliances of
the world, leading statesmen and politicians, important
political ideas and concepts, and crucial events in
world history.

DIRECTORIES AND SOURCES OF
BIOGRAPHICAL INFORMATION

Germany (Federal Republic, 1949-)

Saur, Karl O. Who's Who in German Politics; A Biographical Guide to 4,500 Politicians in the Federal Republic of Germany. New York: R. R. Bowker Co.,
1971. 342p. 72-204749 DD259.63.S28
Gives biographical sketches of each individual listed.

Lawyers--United States

Lawyers Referral Directory. Detroit: National Lawyers
Guild, 1972+ v.1+ 72-620884 KF190.L368
A general directory of lawyers in the United States.

Municipal Government by City Manager

The Municipal Management Directory. Washington, D.C.:
International City Management Association, 1972?+
79-612895 JS344.C5A252
Supersedes the City-Manager Directory. Lists and gives
biographical sketches of current city managers.

Municipal Research--United States

Winston, Eric V. A. <u>Directory of Urban Affairs Informa-</u>
   <u>tion and Research Centers.</u>   Compiled with the cooperation of Marilyn Trezise.   Metuchen, N.J. :   Scarecrow
   Press, 1970.   175p.   79-18109   HT110.W5
   A guide to those organizations, agencies, and institutions engaged in solving urban problems.

Political Science

American Political Science Association.   <u>Directory</u>.
   Washington, D.C. :   American Political Science Association, 1945+   46-48   JA28.A56
   Serving as a "who's who in political science," it gives
   detailed biographical information of members of the
   association.

<u>Current World Leaders; Almanac.</u>   Pasadena, Calif. :
   Almanac of Current World Leaders, 1957+   v. 1+
   No LC card number.
   For each country, lists leading officials down through
   the cabinet level.   Indicates each nation's memberships
   in international organizations.   Published three times a
   year with monthly supplements between issues.

<u>Directory of Political Scientists in Canada.</u>   Montréal,
   Que. :   Société Canadienne de Science Politique,
   1970/71+   v. 1+   72-625592   JA4.D56
   Includes biographical information in English or French.

<u>A Guide to Graduate Study in Political Science.</u>   Washing-
   ton, D.C. :   American Political Science Association,
   1972+   73-645287   JA88.U6G8
   Issued annually gives particulars in graduate institutions
   in the United States.

<u>International Who's Who.</u>   London: Allen & Unwin, 1935+
   v. 1+   35-10257
   Contains biographical data on government leaders, politicians and other personalities who have achieved international fame.

<u>The International Yearbook and Statesman's Who's Who.</u>
   London: Burke's Peerage Ltd. ,   1953+   v. 1+
   53-1425
   Contains brief information on each country.   Has a

separate biographical section containing sketches of approximately 8000 leading world figures in government, business, education and other fields.

Political Science Research--United States

Bibliographic Information Center for the Study of Political Science. Bibliographic Production in Political Science: A Directory. 3d ed. San Jose, Calif.: 1972 17p. 72-195142 JA88.U6B5 1972
A directory of agencies and institutions which have published bibliographies on some phase of political science.

Public Administration

American Society for Public Administration. Membership Directory. Chicago: American Society for Public Administration, 1945+ v. 1+ 68-4323 JA28.A7814
Title varies slightly. Provides short biographical sketches of members.

Haro, Robert P. A Directory of Governmental, Public and Urban Affairs Research Centers at American Colleges and Universities. Davis, Calif.: Institute of Governmental Affairs, University of California, Davis, 1968? 81p. 77-17307 JF1338.A2H35
Lists important agencies and organizations involved in the various areas associated with urban affairs.

Statesmen, American

Biographical Directory of the United States Executive Branch, 1774-1971. Robert Sobel, editor in chief. Westport, Conn.: Greenwood Pub. Co., 1971. 494p. 78-133495 E176.B575
Gives short biographical sketches of each individual.

United States

Who's Who in American Politics. New York: Bowker, 1967/68+ v. 1+ 67-25024 E176.W6424
Includes many biographical sketches of persons active in American politics. Gives education, political position, group membership and other information.

Who's Who in Government. Chicago: Marquis Who's Who, 1972/73+ v. 1+ 72-623344 E747.W512

Supersedes the publication with the same title issued
by the Biographical Research Bureau.   Provides biographical information on important governmental figures.

United States--Officials and Employees

Taylor's Encyclopedia of Government Officials, Federal
    and State.   Dallas: Taylor Pub. Co. , 1967/68+
    v. 1+   67-22269   JK6. T36
    Lists members of U. S. governmental departments and
    agencies, congressional committees, Supreme Court as
    well as federal and state officials of the various states.
    Includes many portraits and viewing charts for con-
    gressional and state senatorial districts.

U. S. Congress

Congressional Pictorial Directory.   Washington: U. S.
    Gov. Print. Off. , 1951+   v. 1+   68-61223rev.
    JK1011. A32
    Title varies.   Provides pictures of Congressional mem-
    bers plus brief biographical sketches.

Congressional Quarterly, Inc.   Members of Congress,
    1789-1970.   Edited by Robert A. Diamond and Arlene
    Alligood.   Washington: Congressional Quarterly, 1971.
    187p.   77-178899   JK1012. Z5   1971
    Lists member of each Congress up to 1970.

Congressional Staff Directory.   Washington, D. C. :   Con-
    gressional Staff Directory, 1959+   v. 1+   69-13987
    JK1012. C65
    A private publication with emphasis on biographical
    sketches and assignments of congressional staff mem-
    bers.

U. S.   Congress.   Biographical Directory of the American
    Congress, 1774-1971, the Continental Congress, Sep-
    tember 5, 1774, to October 21, 1788, and the Congress
    of the United States, from the First through the Ninety-
    first Congress, March 4, 1789, to January 3, 1971,
    Inclusive.   Washington: U. S. Gov. Print. Off. , 1971.
    1972p.   79-616224   JK1010. A5   1971
    Biographical sketches of all persons who have served
    in Congress, plus a listing of members of each Con-
    gress.   Also has a list of executive officers, 1785-
    1971.

U. S.   Congress.   Official Congressional Directory.   Washington: U. S. Gov. Print. Off. , 1809+   v. 1+
6-35330
Includes biographical sketches of Congressmen, their
committee assignments, list of foreign diplomatic rep-
resentatives in the United States, directory of members
of the press accredited to Congress, and much other
information.

ENCYCLOPEDIC WORKS

International Encyclopedia of the Social Sciences.   David
L. Sills, editor.   New York: Macmillan, 1968.   17v.
68-10023   H40. A215
This extensive work is, in effect, a much needed syn-
thesis and summary of the "state of the art" in all of
the social sciences.

Marxism, Communism, and Western Society; A Compara-
tive Encyclopedia.   Edited by C. D. Kernig.   New
York: Herder and Herder, 1972-1974.   8v.   79-176368
AE5. M27
An extensive encyclopedic work in the development and
scope of Communism.

Worldmark Encyclopedia of the Nations.   Editor and Publisher: Moshe Y. Sachs.   4th ed.   New York: Worldmark Press, 1971.   5v.   76-152128   G103. W65   1971
Gives condensed factual information on each country.
v. 1. United Nations. --v. 2. Africa. --v. 3. Americas. --
v. 4. Asia & Australasia. --v. 5. Europe.

HANDBOOKS, MANUALS, ETC.

Alliances

Treaties and Alliances of the World; An International Survey Covering Treaties in Force and Communities of
States.   2d ed.   New York: Scribner, 1974.   235p.
73-15927   JX4005. T72   1974
The bulk of the information can be found in Keesing's
contemporary archives.   A good collection of information on world alliances and treaties.

Cities & Towns

U. S.   Bureau of the Census.   County and City Data Book.
Washington: U. S. Gov. Print. Off. , 1949+   v. 1+
52-4576
Includes more than 100 items of statistical information
for each county, standard metropolitan statistical areas,
and incorporated cities of the United States.

Civil Rights--United States

Adams, A. John.   Civil Rights; A Current Guide to the
People, Organizations, and Events.   With Joan M.
Burke.   New York: Bowker, 1970.   194p.   70-126010
JC599. U5A3468
Includes biographical sketches of important leaders and
organizations engaged in the American civil rights
movement.

Comparative Government

Engle, Eloise K.   National Governments Around the World.
New York: Fleet Press Corp. , 1974.   212p.   72-179013
JF37. E5
A general handbook covering the major governments of
modern nations.   Includes background information and
the structure of each government.

The World This Year.   New York: Simon and Schuster,
1971+   76-649587   JF37. W65
Issued as a supplement to the Political Handbook and
Atlas of the World.   Includes structural, statistical
and leadership data.

Constitutions--Collections

Peaslee, Amos J.   Constitutions of Nations.   Rev. 3d ed.
prepared by Dorothy P. Xydis.   The Hague, M. Nijhoff, 1965+   v. 1+   65-29489   K1. P4   1965
A comprehensive compilation of the constitutions of
foreign countries.

Elections--United States

America Votes; A Handbook of Contemporary American
Election Statistics.   New York: Macmillan, 1956+
v. 1+   56-10132

Presents information by states, on presidential, sena-
torial, congressional, and gubernatorial elections from
the late 1940's to the present.

Petersen, Svend. A Statistical History of the American
Presidential Elections. Introduction: Our National
Elections, by Louis Filler. New York: Ungar, 1968.
250p. 68-57419 JK1967. P4 1968
Contains about 130 statistical compilations, including
table of votes and percentages for each election, for
each state and each historical party, etc.

International Agencies in Europe

Political and Economic Planning. A Handbook of European
Organizations. By Michael Palmer, John Lambert and
others. New York: Praeger, 1969. 519p. 74-6918
JN94. P6 1969
Concise summaries of the structure and activities of
the major European organizations such as the Council
of Europe, NATO, European Economic Community,
etc. Includes membership lists and brief bibliographies.

Legal Research

Pollack, Ervin H. Fundamentals of Legal Research. 3d
ed. Brooklyn: Foundation Press, 1967. 604p.
67-7901 KF240. P6 1967
Discusses the legal research process and the use of
encyclopedias, legal periodicals and indexes, treatises,
etc.

Rombauer, Marjorie D. Legal Analysis and Research.
Seattle: Book Pub. Co., 1970. 161, 28ℓ. 78-140203
KF240. R64
An extensive guide to legal research and the instruc-
tion of law in the United States.

Political Parties--United States

Johnson, Donald B., comp. National Party Platforms,
1840-1972. Compiled with Kirk H. Porter. 5th ed.
Urbana: University of Illinois Press, 1973. 889p.
73-81566 JK2255. J64 1973
Provides the texts of the National party platforms for
the years covered. The only unabridged source for

all of the platforms of American major and minor political parties since 1840.

Political Science

Political Handbook and Atlas of the World. New York:
   Harper & Row for the Council on Foreign Relations,
   1927+   v. 1+   28-12165
   Lists leading government and party officials, gives
   composition of parliament, and lists leading newspapers
   for each country, with their political affiliation.

Public Opinion Polls

Gallup Opinion Index; Report.   Princeton, N.J.: Gallup
   International, 1965+   no. 1+   68-5902   HM261.A1G34
   A monthly compilation of data on responses to Gallup
   Poll questions.   Each issue contains data on about 15
   questions.   Brings together Gallup data otherwise
   scattered throughout many newspapers.

United States--Government Publications

Schmeckebier, Laurence F.   Government Publications and
   Their Use.   With Roy B. Eastin.   2d rev. ed.   Wash-
   ington: Brookings Institution, 1969.   502p.   69-19694
   Z1223.Z7S3   1969
   An extensive guide to U.S. government publications and
   their use.

United States--Politics and Government

Blevins, Leon W.   The Young Voter's Manual; A Topical
   Dictionary of American Government and Politics.   Totowa, N.J.: Littlefield, Adams, 1973.   366p.
   73-10377   JK274.B623
   A modern, topical dictionary of terms related to American government and politics including acts, concepts,
   events, ideas, organizations, personalities, programs,
   and processes.   Entries are alphabetically arranged
   within subject chapters with cross-references.   Also
   included is the complete Constitution of the United
   States, a chapter on Supreme Court decisions, a chapter on federal agencies, and a general index.

Congressional Quarterly Almanac.   Washington: Congressional Quarterly, 1945+   v. 1+   47-41081

Contains a review of the latest congressional session,
a description of major legislation enacted, special reports and voting studies, a survey of lobbying activities,
Supreme Court decisions, etc. , and information on
House and Senate roll call votes.

United States--Statistics

U. S.   Bureau of the Census.   Statistical Abstract of the
United States.   Washington: U. S. Gov. Print. Off. ,
1878+   v. 1+   4-18089
An annual compendium which brings together in one
volume the major statistical sources produced by the
federal government.

INDEXES

Legislation--United States

Congressional Information Service.   CIS Annual.   Washington: Congressional Information Service, 1970+
v. 1+   79-158879   KF49. C62
Issued in 2 pts. :   1. Abstracts of congressional publications and legislative histories. --2. Index to congressional publications and public laws.

Periodicals

Social Sciences Index.   New York: H. W. Wilson, 1907-
15+   v. 1+   17-4969 rev3
Formerly the International Index, 1907-1957; the Social
Science & Humanities Index, 1957-1974.   A subject and
author index to over 200 major scholarly journals in
the Social Sciences.

Social Sciences

Public Affairs Information Service.   Bulletin.   New York:
Public Affairs Information Service, 1915+   v. 1+
16-920 revised.
A wide-ranging subject index to social science materials.   Includes hard to find items.

YEARBOOKS

Commonwealth of Nations

A Year Book of the Commonwealth.   London: H. M.
Stationery Off. , 1969+   v. 1+   79-7332 JN248. C5912
Supersedes the Commonwealth Office yearbook.   In-
cludes a brief history and general statistics of the
Commonwealth.

Communism--Latin America

Yearbook on Latin American Communist Affairs.   Stanford, Calif. : Hoover Institution Press, 1971+   v. 1+
73-177413   HX110. 5. A6Y4
Includes articles on the development of Communism in
Latin American Countries.

Europe--Politics

The Europa Year Book.   London: Europa Publications,
1959+   v. 1+   59-2949
Contains detailed information on European countries
with emphasis upon government.

Great Britain--Foreign Relations

Current British Foreign Policy.   London: Temple Smith,
1970+   v. 1+   72-621051   DA592. C85
Includes documents, statutes and speeches related to
British foreign affairs.

Great Britain--Parliament

The British Political Year.   New York: St. Martin's
Press, 1970+   v. 1+   72-200876   JN101. B7
Includes information on all phases of British political
activity on an annual basis.

International Agencies

Yearbook of International Organizations.   Brussels: Union
of International Associations, 1948+   1st+   49-22132
A reliable and up-to-date source of information on over
150 intergovernmental and over 1200 independent non-
governmental international organizations.

International Relations

Sage International Yearbook of Foreign Policy Studies.
  Beverly Hills, Calif. : Sage Publications, 1973+   v. 1+
  72-98039   JX1291. S25
  Contains discussions of the controversy over the scope
  and method of foreign policy studies; theories of decision-making; the relationship of national public opinion and economic interests to foreign policy; national
  defense policy; and a bibliography of recent foreign
  policy studies.

The Yearbook of World Polity.   New York: Praeger,
  1957+   v. 1+   65-13962   JX68. W6
  A collection of essays on subjects related to international law and organization.   Issued irregularly.   The
  title varies and some volumes have distinctive titles.

Municipal Government

The Municipal Yearbook.   Chicago: International City
  Manager's Association, 1934+   v. 1+   34-27121
  Includes extensive descriptive and statistical data on
  governmental units, personnel, finance, and municipal
  activities.   Includes directories of Mayors and other
  city officers.   Has biographical sections which refer
  to additional sources.

Political Science

Political Science Annual.   Indianapolis: Bobbs-Merrill,
  1966+   v. 1+   66-29710   JA51. P6
  Each volume consists of essays covering current trends
  and research in the field.

The Statesman's Yearbook; Statistical and Historical Annual of the States of the World.   New York: St. Martin's Press, 1864+   v. 1+   4-3776rev2
  An annual containing concise descriptive and statistical
  information on all countries.

Public Opinion--United States

The Harris Survey Yearbook of Public Opinion.   New
  York: Louis Harris and Associates, 1970+   v. 1+
  73-184049   HN90. P8H35
  A compendium of current American attitudes.

Scandinavia--Politics

Scandinavian Political Studies.   New York: Columbia Uni-
    versity Press, 1966+   v. 1+   66-31734   JN7001. S3
    Each annual volume contains substantive essays on gen-
    eral topics in political science and on specific studies
    of Scandinavian politics.

State Governments

The Book of the States.   Chicago: Council of State Gov-
    ernments, 1935+   v. 1+   35-11433
    Produced biennially this work is designed to provide an
    authoritative source of information on the structures,
    working methods, financing and functional activities of
    the various state governments.

United Nations

United Nations.   Yearbook.   New York: Columbia Univer-
    sity Press in cooperation with the United Nations,
    1946/47+   v. 1+   47-7191
    An annual survey of the U. N. and its related agencies
    activities.   Entries are arranged according to political
    and security questions, economic and social questions,
    legal questions, etc.

Chapter Five

THE PERIODICAL LITERATURE

The rapid growth and development of communication in the field of political science identifies itself through the increased production of scholarly books and new scholarly journals reporting on trends in thinking and research. It is estimated that 75 per cent of all printed material is in periodical or serial form. The expansion of the periodical literature poses exciting opportunities for the field of political science. Most obviously, it opens up new channels through which professionals can communicate the results of their thinking and research. The list below includes only the major journals in the field. There are many others, especially those covering a limited subject area within political science.

American Academy of Political and Social Science. Annals. Philadelphia: American Academy of Political & Social Science, 1889+ v. 1+ (bi-monthly) 6-19013 H1.A4 Articles cover most of the current major political and social issues. Each issue is devoted to a single topic. Includes extensive book reviews classified by broad subjects.

The American Behavioral Scientist. Beverly Hills, Calif.: Sage Publications, 1957+ v. 1+ (bi-monthly) 63-24254 H1.A472 Articles stress an interdisciplinary approach to the multiple facets of the social and behavioral sciences. Reports on current research developments.

The American Journal of International Law. Washington:
    American Society of International Law, 1907+   v. 1+
    (Quarterly) 8-36398-7 JX1.A7
    Devoted mainly to contemporary questions of international
    law and relations. Has a cumulative index every twenty
    years.

American Journal of Political Science. Detroit: Wayne
    State University Press, 1957+   v. 1+   (Quarterly)
    73-647828 JA3.M54
    Formerly the Midwest Journal of Political Science. A
    general review of political science. Includes book reviews
    and abstracts of articles contained in each issue.

American Political Science Review. Washington, D.C.:
    American Political Science Association, 1906+   v. 1+
    (Quarterly) 8-9025rev2* JA1.A6
    Contains original articles on all phases of the discipline.
    Includes extensive, detailed, and usually critical book re-
    views.

Arms Control and National Security; An International Journal.
    Croton-on-Hudson, N.Y.: published under the joint aus-
    pices of the Hudson Institute and Pergamon Press, 1968+
    v. 1+   (irregular) 64-62746 JX1974.A1A7
    Title varies: 1968, Arms Control and Disarmament:
    Annual Review. Articles, reviews, factual material, and
    bibliographies in the field of arms control.

British Journal of Political Science. London: Cambridge
    University Press, 1971+   v. 1+   (Quarterly) 70-22767
    JA8.B7
    Presents scholarly articles on most phases of political
    science geared to British interest.

CQ Weekly Report. Washington: Congressional Quarterly,
    Inc., 1945+   v. 1+   (Weekly) 52-36903 JK1.C15
    Weekly reports on major issues, pro-and-con history,
    politics, outlook. Includes many special features related
    to U.S. politics and government.

Canadian Journal of Political Science. Toronto: Canadian
    Political Science Association, Toronto University Press,
    1968+   v. 1+   (Quarterly) 36-11312 JA4.C3
    Includes general articles on political science in both
    French and English. Provides good book reviews. For-
    merly the Canadian Journal of Economics and Political

Science from 1935 to 1968.

Comparative Political Studies.   Beverly Hills, Calif.:   Sage
Publications, 1968+   v. 1+   (Quarterly)   68-7517
JA1. C66
An international journal covering all aspects of compara-
tive politics.   Includes research notes, and an annotated
bibliography.

Comparative Politics.   Chicago: University of Chicago Press,
1968+   v. 1+   (Quarterly)   77-6940   JA3. C67
Presents articles and book reviews devoted to comparative
analysis of political institutions and behavior.   Includes
research notes and book reviews.

The Congressional Digest.   Washington: Congressional Digest, 1921+   v. 1+   (10 issues a year)   23-18526
JK1. C65
Each issue features one major controversy in Congress,
with factual background material and pro-and-con argu-
ments selected from speeches, editorials, articles, testi-
mony before Congressional committees, etc.   Also includes
a news summary "The Month in Congress."

Ethics, An International Journal of Social, Political, and Legal Philosophy.   Chicago: University of Chicago Press,
1890+   v. 1+   (Quarterly)   10-22570 (rev. '40)   BJ1. I6
Contains many scholarly articles related to political
thought.   Includes book reviews, and notes on new books.

Foreign Affairs.   New York: Council on Foreign Relations,
1922+   v. 1+   (Quarterly)   24-9921   D410. F6
Contains scholarly articles on social and political issues,
economics, and all aspects of international affairs.   Includes brief but critical book reviews, there are sections
on source materials and biographical sketches of the contributors.

Foreign Policy.   New York: National Affairs, Inc. ,   1972+
no. 1+   (Quarterly)   73-641825   E744. E75
Provides articles on all aspects of foreign affairs.   Contains no book reviews.

Government and Opposition; A Journal of Comparative Poli-
tics.   London: London School of Economics and Political
Science, Baltimore: Johns Hopkins Press, 1965+   v. 1+
(Quarterly)   65-9983   JA1. G68

An advanced theoretical journal concentrating on the forces
that confront government organization and bureaucracy.
Includes book reviews.

International Affairs.   London: Royal Institute of International Affairs, 1922+   v. 1+   (Quarterly) 39-18471 JX1. A53
Contains scholarly articles analyzing current topics on
politics, economics, and social problems.   Has extensive
book review section and a list of books reviewed.

International Conciliation.   New York: Carnegie Endowment
   for International Peace, 1907+   v. 1+   (5 issues per
year)   8-18491   JX1907. A82
Each issue deals with one particular problem in the field
of international organization and relations, written by a
specialist.   Includes documentary material.   The fall issue of each year deals with the issues before the United
Nations General Assembly.

International Development Review.   Washington: Society for
   International Development, 1959+   v. 1+   (Quarterly)
65-51623   HC10. I6
A readable journal devoted to the economic and political
development of emerging nations.   Includes film reviews
and short book reviews.

International Journal of Politics.   White Plains, N. Y. :
   International Arts & Sciences Press, 1971+   v. 1+
(Quarterly)   71-26367   JA1. A1I59
Covers all areas of political science with translations of
articles published in languages other than English.

International Organization.   Boston: World Peace Foundation, 1947+   v. 1+   (Quarterly)   491752   JX1901. I55
Includes short articles on topics of broad international
scope.   A special feature is "Notes on Theory and Method, " which gives information on ongoing projects using
empirical data.   A selected bibliography is also provided
in each issue.

International Studies Quarterly.   Detroit: Wayne State University Press, 1957+   v. 1+   (Quarterly)   JA1. P58
Articles are concerned particularly with systematic approaches to teaching and research in the field of international relations.   Bibliographic articles are notable for
their thoroughness.

Interpretation; A Journal of Political Philosophy.   The Hague:
   Martinus-Nijhoff, 1970+   v. 1+   (3 issues per year)
   71-21703   JA26.I57
   A scholarly journal devoted to the study of political philosophy.   Contains no book reviews.

Journal of Comparative Administration.   Beverly Hills,
   Calif. :   Sage Publications, 1969+   v. 1+   (Quarterly)
   78-8337   JA3.J65
   Articles cover all phases of public administration.   Has
   occasional book review articles.

The Journal of Conflict Resolution.   Beverly Hills, Calif. :
   Sage Publications, 1957+   v. 1+   (Quarterly)   59-62807
   JX1901.J6
   An interdisciplinary journal which focuses on analysis of
   the causes, prevention, and solution of international, do-
   mestic, and interpersonal conflicts.

Journal of International Affairs.   New York: School of International Affairs, Columbia University, 1947+   v. 1+
   (semi-annual)   50-1537rev.   JX1.C6
   Contains scholarly articles on all aspects of international
   politics.   Has extensive book reviews of a descriptive
   and critical nature.

The Journal of Politics.   Gainesville, Fla. :   Southern Political Science Association, 1939+   v. 1+   (Quarterly)
   41.16606   JA1.J6
   Provides scholarly articles on all aspects of political science.   Excellent and extensive book reviews are included.

Orbis; A Quarterly Journal of World Affairs.   Philadelphia:
   University of Pennsylvania, Foreign Policy Research Institute, 1957+   v. 1+   (Quarterly)   58-4080   D839.068
   Presents well written articles on all aspects of international relations.   Includes a section of book reviews.

Policy Sciences: Policy Analyses, Systems Approaches and
   Decision Making.   New York: Elsevier Pub. Co. , 1970+
   v. 1+   (Quarterly)   79-23541   H1.P7
   Provides articles which will enhance scientific decision methods and techniques of the behavioral sciences, the process
   that humans use in making judgments and decisions.   Includes some book reviews.

P. S. Newsletter of the American Political Science Association.   Washington: American Political Science Association, 1968+   v. 1+   (Quarterly)   JA28. A1P7
Contains news items and articles related to the profession
of political science.   Includes in one issue the doctoral
dissertation in progress and completed in the United States.

Policy Studies Journal.   Urbana, Ill. :   Policy Studies Organization, 1972+   v. 1+   (Quarterly)   72-625926   H1. P72
This journal is designed to provide coverage of various
policy fields from a political science perspective.   Includes no book reviews.

Political Methodology.   Los Altos, Calif. :   Geron-X, Inc. ,
1974+   v. 1+   (Quarterly)   JA1. P58
Contains scholarly articles on methodological approaches
in the field.   Most of the essays present quantitative data.
No reviews are included.

Political Quarterly.   London: Political Quarterly Publishing
Co. , 1930+   v. 1+   (Quarterly)   32-5946   JA8. P72
Provides articles on general political science subjects and
public administration both in England and elsewhere.   Includes excellent book reviews.

Political Science Quarterly.   New York: Academy of Political Science, Columbia University, 1886+   v. 1+   (Quarterly)   7-36315-7   H1. P8
Contains scholarly articles on all aspects of political science.   Includes an extensive, although retrospective,
book review section.

Political Studies.   London: Oxford University Press, 1953+
v. 1+   (Quarterly)   55-28907   JA1. P63
High quality articles on various areas in political science
with particular emphasis on political thought.   Includes
extensive book reviews.

Political Theory.   Beverly Hills, Calif. :   Sage Publications,
1973+   v. 1+   (Quarterly)   73-641963   JA1. A1P64
Contains articles which seek to provide a forum for the
diverse orientations in the study of political ideas.   Book
reviews and book notes are included.

Politics and Society.   Los Altos, Calif. :   Geron-X, Inc. ,
1970+   v. 1+   (Quarterly)   70-23465   H1. P83

Articles are oriented toward research in political behavior
and interdisciplinary studies.   Has a book review section.

Polity.   Amherst, Mass. :   University of Massachusetts,
    1968+   v. 1+   (Quarterly)   77-100   JA3. P65
Articles are international in scope and cover almost all
aspects of the discipline.   Has a book review section.

Public Administration Review.   Chicago: American Society
    for Public Administration, 1940+   v. 1+   (Quarterly)
    A42-2901   JA3. P82
Articles deal with the general problems encountered in
the area of public management and administration.

The Public Opinion Quarterly.   New York: Columbia Univer-
    sity Press, 1937+   v. 1+   (Quarterly)   38-5920
    HM261. A1P8
Articles on public opinion analysis and related subjects,
including voting behavior and propaganda.   Includes book
reviews.

Quarterly Check-List of Economics & Political Science.
    Darien, Conn. :   American Bibliographic Service, 1958+
    v. 1+   (Quarterly)   64-56101   Z7163. Q35
An unannotated bibliographic periodical of recently published books arranged by author or title.

The Review of Politics.   Notre Dame, Inc. :   Notre Dame
    University Press, 1939+   v. 1+   (Quarterly)   40-29523
    JA1. R4
The primary focus of articles in this journal is directed
toward the philosophical and deeper historical meaning of
current events.   Contains a book review section.

SAIS Review.   Washington, D. C. :   School of Advanced Inter-
    national Studies, Johns Hopkins University, 1956+   v. 1+
    (Quarterly)   60-27724   D839. S35
Presents current thought on the theoretical and practical
aspects of international relations as well as news items
regarding the school.

State Government.   Lexington, Ky. :   Council of State Govern-
    ments, 1926+   v. 1+   (Quarterly)   29-25399   JK2403. S7
Articles cover many problems encountered by State governments, written by governors, legislators, and professional political scientists.   Has no book review section.

Studies in Comparative International Development. Beverly
Hills, Calif. : Sage Publications, 1966+   v. 1+   (Month-
ly)   68-7129   H31.S82
Provides monographic material with respect to the politi-
cal, social, and economic aspects of developing nations.
Includes no book review section.

Teaching Political Science. Beverly Hills, Calif. : Sage
Publications, 1973+   v. 1+   (Quarterly)   73-646930
JA88. U6T35
Presents empirical research articles, reports, and essays
which emphasize teaching with direct application to the
subject matter of political science.

UN Monthly Chronicle. New York: United Nations, Office
of Public Information, 1964+   v. 1+   (Monthly)
HX1977. A1V564
Includes articles by distinguished contributors which deal
with various aspects of the work of the United Nations in
all parts of the world.

Urban Affairs Quarterly. Beverly Hills, Calif. : Sage Publications, 1965+   v. 1+   (Quarterly)   65-9957
HT101. U67
Contains scholarly articles on all types of urban problems
including political affairs.   Includes research notes.

Western Political Quarterly. Salt Lake City, Utah: Institute of Government, University of Utah, 1948+   v. 1+
(Quarterly)   51-30582   JA1. W4
Articles cover many international as well as local political problems. Book reviews follow the scope of the journal, concentrating on general works.

World Politics. Princeton, N. J. : Princeton University
Press, 1948+   v. 1+   (Quarterly)   50-3829   D839. W57
Articles deal primarily with problems in international relations and tend to stress concepts and theory. A reviews section incorporates a series of book reviews under
a single topic.

Apter, David E. Anarchism Today 41
Arab Lands of Western Asia, J. J. Malone 41
Arendt, Hannah. Origins of Totalitarianism 109-10
Armacost, Michael H. Foreign Relations of the United States 114
Arms Control and Disarmament 125
Arms Control and National Security 156
Armstrong, John A. European Administrative Elite 100
Art and Practice of Diplomacy, R. B. Harmon 54, 125
Ashford, Douglas E. Ideology and Participation 79
Atherton, A. L. see Jacob, Philip E. 63
Atlantic (Periodical) 26
Audiovisual Market Place 32
Aufricht, Hans. Guide to League of Nations Publications 130
Authority and the Individual, Harvard Tercentenary Conference 43
Authority in the Modern State, H. J. Laski 107

Bachrach, Peter. Political Elites in a Democracy 96
Bailey, Stephen K. Research Frontiers in Politics and Govern-
    ment 91; see Schattschneider, Elmer E. 89
Balandier, Georges. Political Anthropology 60
Barber, Benjamin R. see Friedrich, Carl J. 110
Barber, Sotirios A. Introduction to Problem Solving in Political
    Science 90
Barghoorn, Frederick C. Politics in the USSR 106
Barnett, A. Doek. Uncertain Passage 45
Barros, James. United Nations 111
Bartholomew, Paul C. Public Administration 100; Summaries of
    Leading Cases on the Constitution 114, 122
Bartlett, Sir Frederic C. Political Propaganda 99
Basic Source Materials in Public Administration, R. B. Harmon
    134
Baum, William C. see Wasby, Stephen L. 85
Bayes, John R. see Bollens, John C. 125
Bedau, Hugo A. Justice and Equality 55
Beech, Linda. On the Campaign Trail 54
Beek, Carl, et al. Comparative Communist Political Leadership
    48
Beer, Samuel H. British Political System 60; Modern Political
    Development 49; Patterns of Government 55
Behavioral and Social Sciences Survey Committee. Political Sci-
    ence Panel. Political Science 88
Behavioral Persuasion in Politics, H. Eulau 80
Behavioralism in Political Science, Heinz Eulau 18
Benewick, Robert. Knowledge and Belief in Politics 95
Benne, Kenneth D. Conception of Authority 43
Benson, Oliver E. Political Science Laboratory 86
Bergman, Edward F. see Jackson, William A. D. 60
Berki, R. N. Knowledge and Belief in Politics 95
Berle, Adolf A. Power 97
Bernier, Ivan. International Legal Aspects of Federalism 58
Bertalan, Frank J. Junior College Library Collection 27, 29
Besterman, Theodore. Law: A Bibliography of Bibliographies 139
Between Nothingness and Paradise, G. Niemeyer 110